MARCO ⊕ POLO

THAILAND

CHINA

Tropic of Cancer

MYANMAR
LAOS
Hong Kong

Bay of
Bengal
VIETNAM
South China Sea

THAILAND
Bangkok

Andaman
Islands
(INDIA)
CAMBO-
DIA

Sumatra
(Indonesia) MALAYSIA

www.marco-polo.com

GET MORE OUT OF YOUR MARCO POLO GUIDE

IT'S AS SIMPLE AS THIS

1 go.marco-polo.com/tha

2 download and discover

GO!

WORKS OFFLINE!

SYMBOLS

INSIDER TIP Insider Tip

★ Highlight

●●●● Best of...

☼ Scenic view

Ⓦ Responsible travel: for
ecological or fair trade
aspects

PRICE CATEGORIES HOTELS

Expensive	over 2,900 baht
Moderate	1,450–2,900 baht
Budget	under 1,450 baht

Prices for a double room in
peak season (mid-Novem-
ber–late February)

PRICE CATEGORIES RESTAURANTS

Expensive	over 290 baht
Moderate	145–290 baht
Budget	under 145 baht

Prices for a main course without drinks

On the cover: Chatuchak Weekend Market p. 39 | Rafting in the jungle of Umphang p. 107

MAPS IN THE GUIDEBOOK
(126 A1) Page numbers and
coordinates refer to the road
atlas
(0) Site/address located off
the map
Coordinates are also given for
places that are not marked
on the road atlas
(U A1) refers to the Bangkok
map inside the backcover

(🗺 A–B 2–3) refers to the
removable pull-out map
(🗺 a–b 2–3) refers to the
additional inset map on the
pull-out map

INSIDE FRONT COVER:
The best Highlights

INSIDE BACK COVER:
Bangkok city map

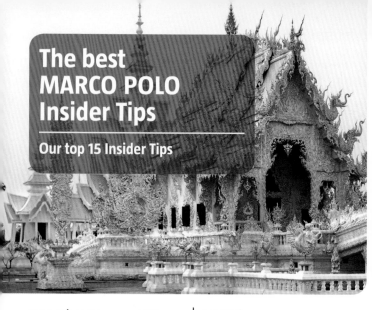

The best MARCO POLO Insider Tips

Our top 15 Insider Tips

INSIDER TIP **Delicious and nostalgic**

The *China Inn Cafe* in Phuket Town is a feast for your eyes as well as your taste buds: the city mansion in Sino-Portuguese style is 100 years old, the Thai cuisine is delicious and the smoothies are to die for → **p. 88**

INSIDER TIP **Beautiful snake path**

Pull out your mobile for great photo opportunities near Pai. The *Bamboo Bridge* stretches over a picturesque landscape of green or, depending on the season you visit, golden rice fields. Buddhist-yellow and Thai blue, white and red flags set the colour tone → **p. 55**

INSIDER TIP **Pure relaxation**

The perfect combination of romance, comfort and a relaxing escape can be found in the paradise that is the *Oriental Kwai* resort near Kanchanaburi. A few days on the river or at the pool, or exploring the area, are just what the doctor ordered! → **p. 43**

INSIDER TIP **Eat like the gods**

Delectable dishes from different culinary worlds are served in the trendy restaurant *Mantra* in Pattaya. The food is as heavenly as the name implies → **p. 71**

INSIDER TIP **Wilderness adventure**

There is no place in Thailand more remote than the *Umphang jungle* on the Myanmar border. The country's most scenic river is ideal for a rafting tour → **p. 107**

INSIDER TIP **Oasis of peace**

At first glance, Hotel *Rachamankha* in Chiang Mai looks more like a temple furnished with antiques than a guesthouse. It's worth popping in, if only for a drink → **p. 50**

INSIDER TIP **Amazing effects**

Become part of a work of art and take an ultimate selfie at *Art in Paradise.* You can literally dive into the fun 3D images at this interactive art museum → **p. 110**

INSIDER TIP Stairway to Heaven
The path is steep: 1,273 steps wind up a mountain from *Wat Tam Sua,* the "temple of the tiger cave", in Krabi. At the top a magnificent panorama awaits → **p. 86**

INSIDER TIP Dining with a temple view
The terrace at *Sala Rattanakosin,* a restaurant near the Grand Palace in Bangkok, provides a stunning view over the Chao Phraya to the Temple of Dawn → **p. 38**

INSIDER TIP A market named Indy
A potpourri of stalls selling everything from jewellery and tacky souvenirs, clothing and cocktails as well as food. No surprise that young locals in Phuket Town flock to the *Indy Night Market* → **p. 88**

INSIDER TIP Luxury bargain
A luxury hotel suite for only about 70 pounds? It's true – if you're travelling upcountry. The *Pullman Hotel* in Khon Kaen is the best place to stay in the Northeast → **p. 58**

INSIDER TIP An artwork in white
Demons, Batman and Buddha -- the *Wat Rong Khun* in Chiang Rai is a whimsical work of art all in white (photo left) → **p. 51**

INSIDER TIP A piece of China amid the tea plantations
Mae Salong in Northern Thailand is home to descendants of the Chinese, who once fled from Mao's army. A cool breeze blows over the coffee and tea plantations, on the market you'll meet the mountain people (photo below) → **p. 51**

INSIDER TIP Temple of three cultures
The *Wat Wang Wiwekaram* in Sangklaburi combines Indian, Burmese and Thai styles to create a masterpiece of temple architecture → **p. 44**

INSIDER TIP Among demons
At the *Sala Kaew Ku* sculpture garden in Nong Khai you have a monumental world of myth and legend almost to yourself → **p. 62**

BEST OF...

GREAT PLACES FOR FREE
Discover new places and save money

FOR FREE

● *The nightly enchantment of ruins*
No admission is charged for the central area of the *Old Sukhothai* temple on weekdays and Sundays after 6pm. As an added bonus, the lighting makes the place seem all the more mystical at night → p. 45

● *Traverse a mangrove swamp on foot*
Why not save the cost of hiring a kayak: on Ko Chang you can walk over the water on the *Mangrove Nature Trail* and see nature up close: mudspringers, monitor lizards and crabs → p. 67

● *Loge seat with a view of the sea*
At Cape Promthep on Phuket, hundreds gather every evening to watch the legendary sunsets. The best views are from the *lighthouse,* which doesn't charge an admission fee → p. 87

● *Sanctuaries by the lake*
Palm trees on a lily pond and two ornate temples that you can visit for free: *Wat Chong Klang* and *Wat Chong Kham* in Mae Hong Son could easily be the setting for an oriental fairytale (photo) → p. 53

● *Phra Nang cave phallic shrine*
On the neighbouring beaches of Railay in Krabi, there are two exceptional caves – and the more bizarre one is free. In *Phra Nang Cave,* hundreds of wooden phalluses stand surrounding a shrine → p. 85

● *The view from the summit of the sublime*
Most places in Thailand frequented by tourists charge admission to see Buddha. But, you can admire the *Big Buddha* on Phuket at no cost and the spectacular view is free, too! → p. 87

● *A charming array of temples*
As you walk through Chiang Mai, you will come across a temple every few minutes that is open to the public for free, including the impressive *Wat Chiang Man* and *Wat Suan Dok* outside of the Old Town → p. 47, 23

(❍ ❍ ❍ ● Dots in guidebook refer to "Best of..." tips

● Water fight!

If you don't like water, then avoid the Thai New Year festival, *Songkran*. During this "water festival" nobody can escape as revellers soak each other with water pistols, hoses, buckets and bowls. It's all great fun – especially in Chiang Mai in northern Thailand (photo) → p. 112

● A house for ghosts

Even the spirits need a home so they don't go out making mischief. So the Thais build little shrines for them, where they leave them offerings. The most famous spirit house in Thailand is the *Erawan Shrine* in Bangkok → p. 22

● Transvestite shows

Nowhere else on earth has such flamboyant transvestite shows as Thailand, complete with their troupes of ladyboys *(kathoeys)*. There costume play is especially spectacularly staged by *Tiffany's Show* in Pattaya → p. 72

● Fighting with fists and feet

Thai boxing is an action-packed sport, involving the use not only of fists but also elbows, knees and feet. The excitement in the ring is matched by the atmosphere in the crowd. The best boxers show off their talents at the *Ratchadamnoen Stadium* in Bangkok → p. 25

● Islands in their thousands

Thailand boasts more islands with gorgeous sandy beaches than anywhere else in Southeast Asia. Whether you're seeking excitement or relaxation, you're bound to find it either in the Gulf of Thailand or the Andaman Sea. A particular unspoiled piece of paradise is *Ko Jum,* where you sometimes encounter more monkeys than tourists on the beach → p. 80

● Nights of culinary delights

When night falls, Thailand is aflame! Every night in the cities you hear gas cookers hissing and see charcoal fires glowing. Food stalls at night markets prepare snacks and entire meals, and they're good places to sample regional specialities – such as the grilled locusts at the *night market in Khon Kaen* → p. 57

ONLY IN

BEST OF...

● *Gather round the wok*
How do you make deliciously creamy curry? What gives the shrimp soup, *tom yam gung,* its hot and sour flavours? Discover the secrets of Thai cuisine at a cooking class at the *Blue Elephant* → p. 39

● *Shopping centres*
It's possible to buy just about anything in Bangkok's shopping centres. The city's most important shopping area is along the Skytrain route. From here you have direct and covered access to shopping centres such as the gigantic *Siam Paragon* (photo) → p. 39

● *Delve into Thailand's history*
Explore the history and culture of the country in a light-hearted way at the *Museum of Siam* -- thanks to sophisticated technology and a good dose of Thai humour → p. 37

● *Unbelievable!*
It might be hard to believe, but *Ripley's Believe It or Not* in Pattaya has a model of the Titanic made of a million matches and a three-legged horse – as well as 300 other bizarre exhibits → p. 70

● *Sharks and other fish*
Is it possible to walk across the sea with dry feet? Yes, but only at *Sea Life Bangkok Ocean World.* Admire the great variety of ocean inhabitants ranging from terrifying sharks and huge crabs to sweet little penguins → p. 110

● *A cinema with a touch of luxury*
As the rain falls outside, snuggle up in your first-class seat at the *SFX Cinema,* the multiplex facility of the Central Festival in Pattaya. Drinks and snacks are brought right to your seat → p. 71

RAIN

RELAX AND CHILL OUT
Take it easy and spoil yourself

● *Massage at the monastery*

Your feet are sore, your neck is stiff – walking around the city can be tiring. Why not seek refuge at a monastery! Treat yourself to a rejuvenating Thai massage at *Wat Pho* in Bangkok, the perfect remedy for your aching muscles → **p. 37**

● *Dinner on the beach*

The sound of the sea, sand trickling through your toes, the smell of grilled fish, and torches and fairy lights everywhere: *Chaweng Beach* on Ko Samui is transformed into an open-air restaurant at night. You won't find a more romantic place to dine → **p. 82**

● *Celestial cocktails hight above Bangkok*

The glass bar glows translucent blue and the city is spread out beneath you as you sip your champagne cocktail. It almost makes you feel you're in seventh heaven. And no wonder: at 220 m (722 ft), the *Sky Bar* in Bangkok has a 360-degree view of the metropolis → **p. 38**

● *Yoga and meditation*

Ko Phangan is renowned for its full moon parties. Yet the island in the Gulf of Thailand is also a place of refuge and a sanctuary for those who wish to learn more about their inner selves. With yoga and meditation you can rediscover body and soul (photo) → **p. 107**

● *All aboard over the Kwai*

Discover life at a slower pace! The leisurely train ride from Kanchanaburi to the sleepy town of Nam Tok follows along the historic tracks of the *Death Railway* over the famous bridge on the River Kwai and a stunning viaduct → **p. 41**

● *Sundowner on the rocks*

The terrace restaurant at the *Rock Sand Resort* on Ko Chang is not much more than a large, rickety shack constructed on an outcrop of rock that provides the foundations. A novel location right on the beach; as you sip your sundowner you can hear the ice tinkle in your glass and the rush of the sea just below → **p. 67**

INTRODUCTION

DISCOVER THAILAND!

A farming village in Northeast Thailand: like a desert island on a vast ocean it stands amidst the *paddy fields*. A monk walks along the dusty village street. An old woman kneels in front of her stilt house and offers the monk her alms: a small plastic bag filled with rice and two hard-boiled eggs. The monk stops and holds out his begging bowl. He does not thank the old woman; it is up to her to give thanks – for having the opportunity to do a good deed. She gets up and climbs the wooden stairs to her house. When she reaches the top, she turns around again. She gazes into the distance, towards where the road loses itself in the rice fields. It leads to *Bangkok*, the big city. Her son works there as a taxi driver. Caught in the capital's morning rush hour, maybe he's the one who buys the chain of jasmine and orchid blossoms from the hawker – a fragrant *good luck charm* to be used as a decoration for his rear-view mirror.

Whether you seek solace in a Thai village or are caught up in traffic in Bangkok, one thing is certain: you are in a country like no other. It is a *land full of secrets*, a strange and exotic place. And yet you won't feel like a stranger for long. It is above all other things the Thai people themselves who have made Thailand the *top travel destination* in Asia. Granted, it is not always easy to understand them: how, for example, can

Photo: Akha women picking tea on the mountain of Doi Mae Salong

Wat Pho, one of the oldest temples in the capital

you fathom a nation which enthusiastically embraces all that is *tansamai* (modern), yet remains highly *superstitious*? The newest smartphone is an indispensable status symbol for many, while the same individuals are afraid of *ghosts* and build miniature houses on every corner – or even entire shrines – to appease the spirits.

The spirits weren't always placated in Thailand, however. Although Thais typically seek harmony, preferring restraint to taking up arms, this was not always the case with their neighbours to the northwest: in 1767 the Burmese invaded and annihilated *Ayutthaya*, one of the most magnificent cities of the age.

When the European powers came to the Far East to divide this part of the world amongst themselves, *Siam* was the only country in Southeast Asia that did not fall under colonial rule. As flexible as bamboo bending with the wind to avoid

8th–11th century
Thais migrate from south-ern China

1238
Sukhothai becomes the capital of the first Thai kingdom

1350
The new kingdom of Ayut-thaya is established

1512
Portuguese traders arrive in Ayutthaya, followed by the Dutch, English and French

1767
Burmese conquer and de-stroy Ayutthaya

1782
King Chakri, Rama I, founds the Chakri Dynasty and proclaims the village

breaking, the nation also strategically manoeuvred itself during the tumultuous years of World War II. Instead of trying to stand up to the far superior forces of the Japanese, they officially became their allies.

The course of Thailand's post-war history was largely decided by *generals*, who regularly came to power on the back of military coups. Student protests in 1973 and 1976 were brutally crushed. But the *economic boom* of the 1980s not only changed Bangkok's skyline, it also had repercussions for the political landscape. The country saw the emergence of a broad-based middle class, which developed a political consciousness and demanded their say. While previously it was students who had taken the streets, the dawn of the new millennium gave rise to *mass protests.*

In 2008 government opponents even occupied the international airport in Bangkok. In 2010, supporters of former Prime Minister *Thaksin*, who had been driven out of office by a military coup, barricaded the main business quarter in Bangkok. The weeks-long protest was violently brought to an end by the military and the police, and almost a

> **Enthusiastic about everything modern, yet deeply superstitious**

hundred people died in the process. After Thaksin's sister *Yingluck* won the election that followed in 2011, it was not long before the next military coup in May 2014, the twelfth successful *coup* since the end of absolute monarchy. Thailand has been governed by General and army chief *Prayut Chan-o-cha* since then.

of Bangkok as the new capital city

1868–1910
King Chulalongkorn, Rama V., sends Thais to be educated in Europe and abolishes slavery

1932
Bloodless coup. Conversion of an absolute monarchy to a constitutional monarchy

1939
Siam is given the name Thailand (Land of the Free)

1946
King Bhumibol Adulyadej is crowned as Rama IX

1997–98
Economic crisis

With an area of 513,120 sq km (198,117 sq mi), Thailand is roughly as large as Spain. Geographically speaking it is divided into four regions. The *Central Plains* with its fertile alluvial soil is renowned as the rice bowl of the country and, along with the metropolis of Bangkok, its economic heart. The *mountains of the North* are the foothills of the Himalayas, where villagers clad in colourful costumes still implement shifting cultivation, and temperatures during winter months are conducive to growing strawberries and apples. The drought-prone plateau of the Northeast comprises almost exclusively farmland, despite the mediocre soil. Around 20 million of the total population of 67 million live in this region, the *Isan*, the poorhouse of the nation, where many villages still have unsurfaced roads and residents get their water from wells or cisterns.

> **In southern Thailand, holiday dreams come true**

Only a few of a whopping 35 million tourists travel to the Northeast. And yet in many ways this region is the most *authentic part* of the country, where the rhythm of life is still determined by sowing and harvesting, by rainy and dry seasons. But who would begrudge a foreigner from a cold climate his preference for a holiday destination where the sea is of a bright turquoise colour and the creamy white beaches make holiday dreams come true: the *South*, which extends down to the Malaysian border. There are fields of pineapple and rows of rubber plantations, coconut palms cast feathery shadows, and fishermen tie colourful scarves and blossom garlands on their boats.

> **Some of the best dive sites in Southeast Asia**

The only Thai city to merit the distinction of "metropolis" is Bangkok. Almost every fourth Thai lives in the commuter belt of the *gigantic capital*. At first glance, Bangkok seems like any other modern city with its skyscrapers, huge shopping malls and bumper-to-bumper traffic. Yet, behind this progressive façade, the traditional *Thai lifestyle* persists. In the streets surrounded by high-rise residential buildings, popular yet simple dishes are sold from food stalls, motorcycle taxi drivers with their bright yellow vests kid around with each other in the shade of an old tree, and people kneel down and pray to Buddha and Hindu gods

2004 A tsunami hits Southern Thailand, killing 5400 people.

2015 A hefty bomb explodes at the Erawan Shrine in the heart of Bangkok, leaving 20 dead and 125 injured in its wake

2016 The highly esteemed King Bhumibol Adulyadej dies in October after his 70-year reign. He was the longest serving Thai monarch

2017 Crown Prince Maha Vajiralongkorn is appointed King after a year of national mourning

before the most modern shopping centres, all reflecting the mix of *tradition and modernity* so typical of Thailand. The provincial cities paint quite another picture. Where lovely wooden houses once stood in most places, you will now only find rather ugly, homogeneous concrete buildings resembling stacked boxes. Only every now and then will you come across *lovely town centres* with old villas and little shops, such as in Phuket Town, Chanthaburi or Lampang.

Even up to World War II most of the kingdom was blanketed by lush greenery: 70 percent of the area was forested. The rapidly growing population, however, has required ever more agricultural land. Today, the *forested area* has dwindled to approximately 20 percent. There are thought to be only 2000 to 3000 wild elephants roaming through the jungle, and the number of endangered big cats

Picture-perfect beach: Phra Nang Beach on the coast of Krabi

is estimated in the hundreds. Their sanctuaries make up only a few of the 120 *national parks* parks, which comprise over half of the remaining forest area in Thailand. Nevertheless, you don't have to go to a zoo to discover Thailand's rich and varied fauna.

The Gulf of Thailand and the Andaman Sea in particular are renowned as having some of the best dive sites in Southeast Asia, though you'll have to be very lucky indeed to see — let alone swim with — a giant plankton-eating *whale shark*. But every dive school knows where to find the spotted (and harmless) *leopard sharks* that you can almost reach out and touch. You won't need a guide to enjoy all the brightly coloured *coral fish* found in these temperate waters. Simply dive down and see!

WHAT'S HOT

1 Flea markets

Totally modern old stuff An increasing number of fashion-conscious Thais are heading to the flea markets to find trendy vintage clothes, furniture and antiques. The best are held in Bangkok where you can stroll along looking for odds and ends as well as a good bargain or two. At the *Chatuchak Weekend Market (photo)* (see p. 39) and the "railway market" *New Talad Rod Fai (Thu–Sun 5pm–midnight | Ratchadaphisek Rd | eastern part of the city)*, even those who hate shopping will be delighted by vintage and retro stuff, live bands, street food and many photo opportunities.

2 Get the kick!

A ball on the rise Sepak Takraw, the fast-paced mix of volleyball, football and athletics is becoming a national sport in Thailand. It not only involves long passes over a net with the woven ball but also rather artistic overhead kicks come into to play. It's interesting to watch and fun to play. Regular matches of the Thai league take place all over the country. The *National Stadium* in Bangkok is one of the sport's most important venues.

3 Progressive

Thai music Indie musicis a not a genre that one would necessarily associate with Thailand. However, there is a lively and very popular scene. You can listen to the Thai rock sound both live and as background music in the pubs around Bangkok's Thammasat University, such as the *Phra Nakorn Bar & Gallery (58/2 Soi Damnoen Klang Rd)* or the *Good Story (72–74 Phra Athit Rd)*.

Food trucks

Everything on wheels The modern version of the beloved street food stall has been put on wheels in converted mini buses or pick-ups. Trucks selling American-style juicy burgers are all the rage at the moment in Bangkok. People queue up in front of the trucks belonging to *Mothertrucker (Tue–Sun | usually near Khao San Rd and at Central World | www.fb.com/mothertruckerbkk)* and *Orn The Road (daily | usually Soi Nana, Chinatown| www.fb.com/orntheroad bkk)*. But some of the good old food stalls are also enjoying a comeback. Ever since the 72-year-old street food queen, Supinya Junsuta, received the first Michelin star ever to be awarded in Thailand at the end 2017, tables at her Chinatown cookshop *Raan Jae Fai (Mon–Sat | 327 Mahachai Rd | tel. 0 22 23 93 84)* have been booked out weeks in advance.

Weekend trips

Explore Thailand by plane Since the emergence of discount regional airlines such as *Air Asia (www.airasia.com) (photo), Nok Air (www.nokair.com)* or *Lion Air (www.lionairthai.com),* flights have become cheaper and more convenient than ever before. Domestic flights hardly cost more than the corresponding coach trip, but they are much faster and give the residents of Bangkok a chance to escape the metropolis for the weekend. As a result, the traditional day trip destinations near the capital are facing stiffer competition: not only the tourist hot spots, but also smaller cities such as Nan, Khon Kaen or Loei are attracting an increasing number of Thai tourists on Saturdays and Sundays.

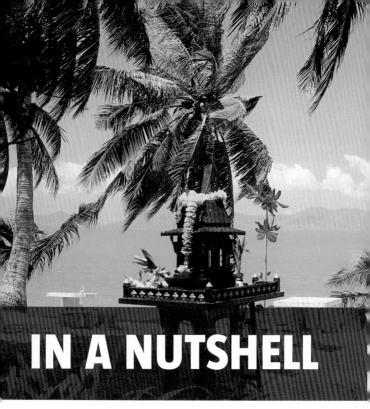

IN A NUTSHELL

AMULETS IN THEIR DOZENS

All Thais know that misfortune lurks around every corner. That's why they arm themselves with amulets to ward off evil. Amulets are customarily small figures of Buddha or images of famous monks, which Thais hang around their necks – the more massive the gold chain, the better the protection. People with particularly hazardous occupations such as bus drivers will garland themselves with as many as a dozen such good luck charms. Amulets are of course only effective if a monk has blessed them. Although the ritual does not really adhere to Buddhism, Thais are not averse to mixing faith with superstition.

CULTURAL FAUX-PAS

In Thailand, it's easy as a foreigner to commit a gaffe or faux-pas. Just imagine in England, you'd never dream of eating fish and chips with a spoon or shaking hands with a waiter when he takes your order. So there: Thai rice dishes are preferably eaten with spoons and forks and not with chopsticks. The noodle soup is the only exception; it is eaten with both a spoon and chopsticks. And the graceful gesture of the Thais known as a *wai,* where both hands are put together in front of the chest, should be reserved for those who have, according to Thai rules of etiquette, "earned" it. This means, in the bluntest terms, waiters, children and beggars are not greeted with the *wai.*

Thais understand how to worship spirits, eat insects and have fun. And good manners are appreciated by everyone

And the higher the social status of the person being greeted and the older they are, the higher you'll have to lift your hands – with an abbot or monk, your fingertips are almost touching their forehead and you bend slightly forwards. If you're unsure of the correct etiquette, simply smile and nod politely. Kids can be greeted with the international "hello".

Thais are tolerant and don't meddle in other people's affairs, However, there are situations where tolerance reach-es its limits, such as when derogatory remarks are made about the Royal Family or Buddhism, its followers and symbols. Shoes must be removed in temples (not applicable to Chinese temples), mosques and private residences. Women are not allowed to touch monks, and are also not permitted to sit beside them on buses. Not paying attention to your appearance means you lose face. Temple visits or appointments with authorities require appropriate attire. Failing to adhere to the strict dress code may result in being denied admission or poorly served – or not served at all. Topless bathing is a violation against local customs. Anyone who displays anger openly is similarly reviled: for Thais, the loss of self-control is one of the worst human characteristics. The head is not regarded as "sacred", as some Westerners think, but figuratively, as well as literally, it is the highest part of the body. A foreigner should not touch a local's head, even if it is meant in a friendly way. The soles of the feet are the lowest part of the body, and must not be shown to anyone. Be careful to never point your feet at someone else, especially at a Buddha statue in a temple.

HAUNTED HOUSES

Even though they might be devout Buddhists, the world of the Thais is full of *phii*, spirits. The spirits must have their own house to stop them from wandering about and creating mischief – small and plain like a birdhouse, or as grand and opulent as a temple. The invisible neighbours are always pleased with the gifts bestowed on them by mortals: flowers, rice, a glass of water, and on important days, a fried chicken.

And it works, guaranteed! The ● *Erawan Shrine* on the corner of Ploenchit Rd/Ratchadamri Rd in Bangkok is famous throughout Thailand: When the Erawan Hotel (now the Grand Hyatt Erawan) was being built in the 1950s, there was a spate of fatal accidents. In order to appease the spirits dwelling in the structure, a shrine was built. From that day on, no more workers were killed. Unfortunately, the Erawan Shrine also made international headlines in August 2015 when a bomb exploded, killing 20 people and injuring 125 others.

ELEPHANT TOURISM

The issue of tourists and elephants in Asia is an extremely controversial one. Domesticated elephants are used primarily for commercial purposes and are an extremely lucrative business. The elephants are paraded around the streets for stroking and feeding, used in elephant camps, lend their backs to jungle trekkers and even amuse visitors at shows with their ability to paint and play music. You can even train to be a Mahout in a several-day course and earn your "elephant riding licence". There is no dividing line between putting the ageing jumbos out to rest and using them as toys to amuse tourists. It is advisable to stay away from the circus shows which often make the creatures perform cruel tricks.

Elephants have been part of life in Asia for thousands of years and superstition surrounds these animals. This makes the

Buddha is omnipresent in Chiang Mai, a city with over 300 temples

issue far more complicated than some animal welfare activists in the Western world would like you to believe who criticise all types of elephant activity per se. However, a reversal in trend is in sight: The first travel operators have taken up the mantle and have removed visits to elephant shows from their itinerary. If you should book a safari tour which includes a visit to the elephants, make sure to take a closer look at their living conditions or contact the relevant animal welfare organisations for more information before you go.

IN THE NAME OF BUDDHA

An estimated 94 percent of Thais are Buddhist. Even today, it is common for young men in rural areas to spend at least a few days, if not weeks or months, in a monastery. In Buddhism, life means hardship, caused by desires like a craving for material possessions. Yet the pursuit of affluence has itself become a religion, to which even monks and monasteries have succumbed. Some novices even take money rather than food in their begging bowls, which is something they should not strictly do. An amazing opportunity to interact with Buddhist Monks and learn more about Buddhism is through *monk chats:* In Chiang Mai, you can try out *Wat Chedi Luang* (see p. 48) or ● *Wat Suan Dok (Suthep Rd | free admission).*

ABOUT TEMPLES

Wat is the term for a temple, but it can also refer to the entire monastery compound. Monasteries are often found in conjunction with temples. The prayer hall of a wat is called a *bot;* the *chedi* is a bell-like tower whereas a classic Khmer-style stupa is known as a *prang.* Visitors to these sacred buildings places should wear appropriate clothing, making sure to cover their shoulders and knees – a rule which applies to both men and women. A sarong wrapped around the shoulders will also suffice if you have nothing else suitable. Shoes must be left at the entrance to the main sanctuary. Do not pose for selfies with and on the Buddha figures and do not sit with your feet pointing toward the Buddha.

TASTY BUGS

Eyes closed, mouth open and swallow! What for some in the Western world is a disgusting dare is in Thailand a delicacy, especially in the north and northeast of the country. By doing so, Thais are in trend because insects are completely organic, sustainable and, what's more, available in abundance. They are also healthy – rich in protein – and are even said to have aphrodisiac qualities.

The insects are not consumed raw; the fresh animals are thrown into the wok and served with a sprinkling of salt, chilli or kaffir lime leaves. Taste buds tickled? Then start by trying the crispy fried locusts. Grasshoppers *(ta ka tan)* or the fattier crickets *(jing reed)* taste similar to popcorn or pretzels. Or why not go for red ants *(mod daeng)* or their eggs and larvae? Some mouths will literally water simply at the thought of water bugs *(malaeng da na,* often confused with cockroaches, similar to chicken in texture), silk worms *(nhon mhai,* nutty taste) and bamboo caterpillars *(rod duan).*

You can walk from stall to stall tasting these specialities at most street markets. Some gourmet restaurants are now also serving these six and more legged creatures which have never been cheap. A bag of bugs usually costs around 0.50

pence, the deep-fried scorpions £1.70 at Bangkok's INSIDER TIP ▶ *Klong Toey Market* or on the *Khao San Road.*

NO PLASTIC BAG, PLEASE!

The environmental protection movement in Thailand is still in its infancy. Ancient buses belch forth their filthy fumes, raw sewage flows into the rivers and seas, and people seem to chuck their litter anywhere they like. But there is a light at the end of the tunnel: entire school classes go out and collect litter from kerbsides, squares and beaches. Diving schools regularly organise underwater clean-ups, and tourists are welcome to help rid coral reefs of old nets, bottles, and other garbage. Here and there campaigns have been launched to promote jute instead of plastic bags and on Ko Samui old mopeds are transformed into expensive works of recycled art and furniture. Tourists can also do their bit to reduce waste by not taking a plastic bag to carry even the smallest purchases – similar to the coffee-to-go cups found everywhere back home.

SANUK – AND WHERE THE FUN ENDS

Sanuk, often translated as meaning "having fun", is a way of life in Thailand. The country is known as the Eldorado for sex tourists from around the world – a multi-million dollar business in which brothels masquerade as go-go bars, karaoke clubs and massage parlours. It's hard to believe but prostitution is actually illegal in Thailand if it is displayed "openly and shamelessly". Yet visit the reputed streets in Bangkok, Pattaya or Phuket and you will see first-hand how "effective" the law is. Decades of double standards brought new legislation to Thailand in 1996 targeted at curtailing the sexual abuse of children: Sex with minors under 18 years of age is taboo and carries a penalty of up to three years in prison. Anyone charged with the abuse of children under 15 faces imprisonment for up to 20 years in the notorious Thai prisons as well as prosecution under UK law.

One sight which leaves many visitors in awe is the country's *kathoeys*, or ladyboys. The most beautiful of these transvestites perform in lavish shows at the main tourist resorts. Many of the other 230,000 transvestites and transsexuals in Thailand also have "regular" jobs such as shoe sellers or bookkeepers to earn a living. If you are approached by a bar lady with a large bosom and you are unsure if she is a ladyboy, look for a protruding Adam's apple.

POTPOURRI THAILAND

Thailand is a melting pot of tribes and nations which have settled here over the centuries. Around 67 million people to be precise, a quarter of which are immigrants from the poorer neighbouring countries such as the Khmer from Cambodia, Laotians from Laos, Shan and Mon from Myanmar, the Vietnamese and not forgetting in the deep South the Muslims from Malaysia and the many Chinese ancestors of ethnic Thais.

Particularly colourful are the *chao kao,* the peoples of the mountains. There are an estimated half a million tribe members, some of whom still wear their traditional costumes today – at least when tourists from around the world come to visit their villages. The women from the Akha, Lisu, Lahu and Meo (also referred to as Hmong) are particularly photogene. Centuries ago, the mountain tribes grew poppies for the manufacture of opium. Today they prefer to

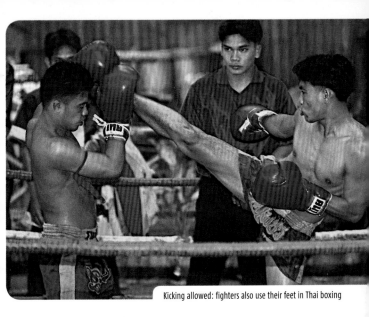

Kicking allowed: fighters also use their feet in Thai boxing

"deal" in souvenirs and earn their living with the cultivation of fruit, vegetables and flowers, coffee and tea. Avoid visiting the Padaung tribe in the villages of the "long neck" or "giraffe neck women" whose necks are stretched to unnatural lengths by means of brass rings. Only rich businesspeople make a profit from this "human zoo".

TRENDY MUAY THAI

Several times a week, the air is burning at the ● *Ratchadamnoen Stadium(Mon, Wed, Thu, Sun | 1 Ratchadamnoen Nok Rd | www.rajadamnern. com)* in Bangkok: The national sport *Muay Thai* uses gloved fists, but also the feet. To heighten the excitement matches are accompanied by drums. Notorious gamblers, Thais never pass up the chance of a bet, especially during a fight. This centuries-old martial art demands a certain level of fitness:

You can learn the right kick with 15 different basic techniques in the popular training camps geared at foreigners in many holiday resorts on Ko Phangan.

CONFUSING WORDS

Are you, white stranger, a *falang* or a *farang*? How to write this Thai denomination for all foreigners (where the word maybe derives from)? Are you on holiday in Ko Samui or Koh Samui? *Ko(h)* means island, but why are there two ways to spell it? Why is a beach sometimes *hat*, in other instances *had* and sometimes written as *haad*? There is no straight answer. To foreigners, the Thai script is akin to a book with seven seals, written in graceful yet unintelligible squiggles. And there is no hard-and-fast rule for transcribing these lines into Latin characters.

FOOD & DRINK

Thai food is not only considered among the best in the world, it is also exceptionally healthy. It is inimitable and distinctive, yet influenced especially by Chinese, Indian and Malaysian cuisine.

Eateries steam and sizzle on every corner. Street vendors sell grilled squid, kebabs, and ice-chilled fruit. Mobile *food stalls* set up at the roadside, a few chairs and a table occupy the pavement, the open-air restaurant is ready for business.

Whether done over a hissing gas stove or charcoal, the food will be delicious: *noodle soup* with chicken or duck, fried rice with crab, an omelette with mussels or pancakes with pineapple. Meat is used in abundance; poultry and seafood are also likely to be a part of the meal. Vegetables are cooked al dente to retain their vitamins. Various *spices and herbs* such as coriander, lemongrass and lemon leaves, Thai ginger and basil, tamarind, mint, curry and shrimp paste give Thai food its signature zest. And don't forget the garlic and chillies!

Only upmarket *restaurants* keep to strict mealtimes such as lunch (around 11.30am–2pm) and dinner (around 6–10pm). Most establishments will carry on serving until late at night and hot food stalls in the larger cities and tourist centres are open virtually around the clock. If not otherwise stated, all restaurants mentioned in this guide are open daily.

Photo: *Tom yam gung*, a classic Thai dish

Thai cuisine is often spicy, yet always light – and for dessert, a heavenly selection of fruit awaits

Thai dishes are served in bite-sized portions or are easily cut with a spoon and fork. Held in the right hand, the spoon is used for eating, while the fork serves only to slide the food onto the spoon. Only noodle dishes and soups are eaten with *chopsticks*, which have been inherited from the Chinese. A typical Thai meal to go round a group consists of up to five *flavours*: bitter, sweet, sour, salty and hot. Meals are served with a big bowl of rice. Dishes can be eaten in any order and every-

one just tucks in. Usually, only one dish (with rice) is put on the plate at the start of the meal. Only when it is finished comes the next dish for you to taste. This way, the different tastes don't mix on the plate.

Thais use generous amounts of *chili*, though in tourist restaurants they tend to be used more sparingly. To err on the side of caution, you can state your preference for *mai peht* (not spicy). Guests can season standard dishes such as fried rice, fried noodles

gaeng kiau wan gai – green curry with chicken and aubergine, slightly sweet *(wan)*

gaeng massaman – red curry with strips of beef, peanuts and potatoes (mildly hot), especially popular in Southern Thailand (photo left)

gung hom pa – battered shrimp, especially tasty when dipped in tartare sauce or a sweet and sour vinegar sauce with sliced chilli

kao niau – sticky rice, a favourite in Northeastern Thailand to accompany spicy salads

kao pat – fried rice with egg *(kai)* and vegetables *(pak)*. Other ingredients are crab *(gung)*, pork *(mu)* or chicken *(gai)*

kui tiao nam – noodle soup, usually made with pork or chicken, but especially tasty with duck *(pet)*. Thailand's favourite snack (photo right)

nam tok – a spicy salad with strips of beef *(nuä)* or pork and plenty of fresh herbs mixed with ground roasted rice

plamuk tohd katiam pik thai – strips of squid, fried with garlic and pepper (not hot)

som tam – salad made of thin strips of green papaya, with cocktail tomatoes, dried shrimp, fish sauce and lots of chillies. Raw vegetables, sticky rice and grilled chicken *(gaiyang)* go well with this dish

tom kha gai – soup made with chicken and coconut milk, a particularly exotic treat. Caution: the broth also contains chilli peppers!

tom yam gung – sour shrimp soup with lemongrass and lots of chillies. Thailand's unofficial national dish

yam wunsen – glass noodle salad with herbs, shrimp and ground pork. Caution: chillies give this salad its bite!

or noodle soup themselves: each table has its own small container with dried and ground chilli peppers, sugar (for the noodle soup) as well as a sweet-and-sour vinegar containing pieces of chili. *Nam pla,* a light brown liquid made from fermented fish is used instead of salt. When substituted with chopped chillies, it's known as *pik nam pla* – don't use too much!

Salads are not like Western-style salads. A typical **Thai salad (yam)** is more like a main dish and is eaten as a snack. And it is nearly always very spicy! The hearty *yam nua,* for example, is a slightly sour tasting salad with stir-fried beef strips, garnished with garlic, coriander, onion and crushed chilli peppers. Another popular dish is *yam wunsen,* which features glass noodles as its main ingredient.

Thais love their **sweets**, sweet being the operative word. The small calorie-rich desserts are found in every colour of the rainbow at food stands at festivals, on markets and from street vendors. Especially popular are the delicious treats made of sticky rice wrapped in banana leaves and cooked in coconut milk.

Thailand is an oasis for **exotic fruit**. To Thais, the durian (famous for its odour) is the "king of fruits". The pale yellow flesh under its thorny husk is almost like custard; you're either addicted straight away or put off forever. The mango *(mamuang)* goes especially well with concentrated coconut milk and sticky rice. Thais also adore green mango strips, which they dip into a mixture of sugar and chillies. Beneath the wine-red peel of the mangosteen *(mangkut)* lies a delicate white, juicy fruit that has both a sweet and somewhat sour taste. Also try the hairy rambutan*(ngo),* the fine lychees *(lintshi)* or the bell-shaped red Java apples *(djompu).*

The selection of freshly-squeezed **fruit juices** on markets is also very varied. Bottled drinking water *(nam plao)* and mineral water is available everywhere. The most popular local **beer** is *Chang.* Other beer brands brewed in Thailand are Heineken, Tiger, and Singha. The inexpensive rums, *Mekhong* and

Dining under palm trees is on everyone's agenda in Thailand

Saeng Som, are distilled from sugar cane and marketed as *"whisky".* They are not served neat but as a long drink with soda water. Tourists often enjoy this beverage mixed with Sprite or cola.

SHOPPING

It's worth keeping an eye open for more original souvenir ideas than the usual tourist stuff. Shoes, brand-name drugs, spices and clothing are often available at a fraction of the cost that you would pay back home. Department stores have fixed prices, and many individual shops and stores in shopping malls display their prices too, but it is still possible to negotiate there. Haggling with street vendors is compulsory and it can also be lots of fun if you enjoy the banter and jokes that go along with it.

If you buy goods with a value of at least 5,000 baht (show your passport!) and spend a minimum of 2,000 baht per transaction, you can have the VAT reimbursed upon departure at the airports in Bangkok, Hat Yai, Chiang Mai and Phuket. However, it's only worth the effort for amounts over 20,000 baht.

ANTIQUITIES & BUDDHA STATUES

Antiques as well as Buddha statues, even newly made ones, require an export licence, and a reputable business will organise this for you; the body responsible for licences is the *Department of Fine Arts* (tel. *0 22 25 26 25*) in Bangkok. The export of historical Buddha figures is generally prohibited. Genuine Thai antiques are rare, so dealers will often stock items originating from many Asian countries, such as Chinese porcelain or historical maps from colonial times. Caution: an entire industry in Thailand has been built on passing off new wares as antiques.

COSMETICS

Just follow your nose! Cosmetics are usually located on the ground floor in department stores, often occupying the entire floor space. Thai women adore perfumes, creams, etc, and the choice of products is correspondingly huge.

CUSTOM-MADE CLOTHING

Arrange at least one fitting with the tailor and don't be afraid of requesting alterations, if necessary. A deposit is usually required, but make sure you're completely satisfied with your garment before paying the balance.

Whether you're looking for pearls or perfume, stylish accessories or made-to measure clothing: Thailand makes shopping fun

FASHION & ACCESSORIES

In Thailand you can find brand-name fashion from all over the world. But local designers are increasingly creating a stir with their creations. Bangkok is by far the best shopping destination for fashion chic: in the enormous shopping centres and department stores, shopping sprees are difficult to resist.

GOLD & JEWELLERY

Never buy jewellery from a street vendor; and don't let yourself be lured into shops by pushy touts! Gemstone scammers, who work with dubious jewellers, lie in wait for naive tourists near the main attractions in Bangkok in particular. Gold jewellery up to 23 Karat is available in special gold shops, which you will recognise by their red interior. Prices are based on the current gold price plus approx. 10 percent for processing.

PEARLS

Thailand's cultivated pearls come from the waters off the island of Phuket in the South. It's possible to visit farms to learn about how the precious gems grow in their oyster shells.

PIRATE COPIES

Be it Rolex or Gucci – pirate copies are available for brand names and anything that is costly. You will have no trouble with the Thai police purchasing such items, but it may be a different story with customs officials when you get home: you are only allowed one forged product!

SILK

Since traditional Thai silk is hand woven, each silk fabric is unique. It is never completely smooth, having a slightly coarse feel that makes it warm and vibrant to touch but doesn't diminish its elegance.

CENTRAL THAILAND

The water of the Chao Phraya and its tributaries has made the alluvial plain north of Bangkok the most important rice-growing region in the country. The paddies, where succulent green shoots spring up at the beginning of the rainy season, stretch towards the horizon.

Sukhothai marks the beginning of northern Thailand. It is also where, in 1238, the Thai nation was born with the founding of the first capital city. A century later, Ayutthaya, the second royal city, rose to power. But both had to learn from Buddha's teachings: "Nothing is permanent". Today, their ruins tell us of their glorious past. The modern capital Bangkok is a world metropolis. Only two hours to the west, however, in the province of Kanchanaburi, an entirely different landscape awaits: past the fields and wasteland, jungle-covered hills and mountains suddenly appear. Close to the border of Myanmar the land is raw, wild and only sparsely inhabited. Nevertheless, here you can visit another chapter of history: the world-famous Bridge over the River Kwai and the "Death Railway" are enduring reminders of World War II.

AYUTTHAYA

(131 D5) (*ш D8*) **The rivers of Chao Phraya, Pasak and Lopburi flow around the historic core of the city of 60,000 inhabitants ★ Ayutthaya.**

Ancient royal cities and a world metropolis: from the Cradle of Siam via Bangkok to the wild frontier of the Three Pagoda Pass

Its strategic, slightly hidden island position, which it still holds today, helped the city to become a prospering trading post from the 14th to the 18th century. It was the longest Siamese kingdom to be in existence, lasting four centuries with 33 kings. This gem of an old town is today a Unesco World Heritage Site (since 1991). The historic centre is dotted with ruins of temples and palaces whose columns, pillars and towers still dominate the city's skyline.

SIGHTSEEING

The individual attractions cost 20–150 baht each per admission, there is also a combination ticket for 230 baht (with six temple sites to choose from). Normal opening times are 8am–6pm although some sites are only open until 4.30pm.

ANCIENT PALACE

This is where the kings resided, in the Wang Luang close to the north-western section of the city wall, but only a few ruins attest to that today. A royal temple *(Wat Phra Si Sanphet)* stands in the palace grounds; its three massive, restored chedis are Ayutthaya's landmark. Inside this beautiful ensemble, the ashes of three kings are kept. *Daily 8am–6pm | admission 50 baht*

Deeply rooted: Buddha head at Wat Mahatat in Ayutthaya

AYUTTHAYA HISTORICAL STUDY CENTER

If the history of this ancient city is leaving you slightly confused, this study centre provides a good introduction to the Ayutthaya kingdom as well as to the lives of their kings and villagers with exhibitions and models. An audio-visual guided tour takes you around the Ancient Palace (which is refreshingly cool inside) in its full splendour before it was destroyed by the Burmese in 1767. *Daily 9am–4pm | admission 100 baht | Rojana Rd | south of Phraram Park*

INSIDER TIP WAT CHAI WATTHANARAM

It's worth venturing to the opposite banks of the river to visit this impressive, photogenic and symbolic temple, steeped in mythology and in a fine state of preservation. The 35 m/115 ft-high Khmer-style central *prang* instantly transports you to Angkor in Cambodia. It is surrounded by eight smaller pointed chedis. It symbolises the most sacred of all mountains, the Meru, at the centre of the Hindu-Buddhist universe. You are literally walking through the home of the Gods along towers, galleries and brick walls adorned with more than 100 Buddha statues. *Daily 8am–6pm | admission 50 baht | on the western bank of the Chao Phraya river outside of the old town island*

WAT MAHATAT

This enormous temple complex located on the eastern edge of Phraram Park in the old city centre *(daily 8am–6pm | admission 50 baht)* is perhaps Ayutthaya's most striking monument. As you walk around the perimeter wall, don't miss the iconic image of the severed Buddha head cradled in the roots of a massive banyan tree. At night, the complex is even more majestic under the floodlights.

FOOD & DRINK

Try the local fare at the food stands at the night market *Hua Ra* by the river or the stands in Phraram Park. For a tasty but cheap noodle soup, head northeast of Wat Mahathat to *Ang Lek Noodle*

(Chikun Rd), which is always busy at lunchtime.

BANGKOK

WHERE TO STAY

BAAN TEBPITAK

Friendly, family-run guesthouse with comfortable rooms, a bungalow and a pool. *10 rooms | 15/19 Pathon Rd, Soi 3 | mobile tel. 08 98 49 98 17 | www.baan tebpitak.com | Budget–Moderate*

KANTARY HOTEL

Suites wherever you look: the chic hotel offers serviced apartments with all the amenities at a good price and a pool. *174 rooms | Rojana Rd | tel. 0 35 33 71 77 | www.kantarycollection.com | Expensive*

INFORMATION

TOURISM AUTHORITY OF THAILAND
Si Sanphet Rd | tel. 0 35 24 60 76

MAP INSIDE THE BACK COVER
(131 D5–6) *(⚏ D9)* **Although the international usage "Bangkok" has prevailed, Thais prefer to call their capital city (pop. approx. 9 million) by its more beautiful name: Krungthep, "City of Angels".**

The best way to get around the city quickly and cheaply is by the elevated Skytrain (BTS). Two underground metro lines (MRT) operate e.g. between the central station via Silom Road and Sukhumvit Road and to Chatuchak Weekend Market. The inexpensive *Day Pass* is valid for the whole day and costs 120–140 baht. The blue *Chao Phraya Tourist Boats (daily 9am–6pm | hop-on-hop-off day ticket approx. 180 baht | www.chaophrayatou ristboat.com))* ferry you to many of the attractions along the river of the same name. Diverse ferries and express boats also offer their services *(daily 6am–7pm | www.chaophrayaexpressboat.com).*

★ **Ayutthaya**
In the old royal city on the trail of the "Golden Age": the ruins recall ancient splendour and greatness and have done so for 600 years → p. 32

★ **Grand Palace and Wat Phra Kaeo**
You absolutely must visit this majestic complex in old Bangkok and admire the unique whimsical architecture → p. 36

★ **Chatuchak Weekend Market**
Go bargain hunting at this superlative flea market in Bangkok: find whatever your heart desires at one of over 10,000 stands → p. 39

★ **Sangklaburi**
An adventure tour to the Three Pagodas Pass in the wild frontier → p. 44

★ **Death Railway**
A journey along the infamous stretch of track, from the world-famous bridge on the Kwai to the end station, Nam Tok → p. 41

★ **Old Sukhothai**
Travel back in time to the birth of a nation: Sukhothai was the first Thai capital city. Today, the graceful ruins are reminiscent of the "Dawn of happiness" → p. 45

MARCO POLO HIGHLIGHTS

Almost too big for shelter is Wat Pho's exquisite highlight, its reclining Buddha

SIGHTSEEING

GRAND PALACE AND WAT PHRA KAEO
⭐ (U A3–4) (*m a3–4*)

The *royal palace,* with its *Temple of the Emerald Buddha (Wat Phra Kaeo),* is the most famous historic site in Thailand. Behind their whitewashed walls, the various structures, crowned by intricate roof details and shiny golden spires, have a magical appeal. Demons and mythical creatures watch over the complex, while splendid murals recall life in the royal court and the life of Buddha. The Emerald Buddha in the Royal temple is actually made of jadeite rather than emerald, and is only 66 cm high, yet it is regarded as a national shrine. Tourists can only get in wearing appropriate attire; short or very loose trousers, miniskirts, leggings, shoulder-free tops and sandals open at the back are frowned upon. Appropriate clothing can be borrowed for a fee. Admission also entitles you to visit the *Royal Decorations and Coin Pavilion* and the *Ananta Samakhom throne hall* (U C2) (*m c2*). *Daily 8.30am–4pm | admission 500 baht | Na Phralan Rd | www.palaces.thai.net*

> ### 🏙 WHERE TO START?
> **Sanam Luang (U A3) (*m a3*):** The large open space is a perfect starting point for exploring the historical city centre. The Grand Palace, Wat Pho and Museum of Siam are only a few steps away, and the Old Town area of Banglamphoo are within five minutes' walk. The Sanam Luang (royal square) is served by bus routes 25, 507 and 508. Nearest public transport stations: Hua Lamphong metro; Skytrain: National Stadium.

KLONG (U A–B 4–6) (*m a–b 4–6*)

In the district of Thonburi, both people and goods are still transported on the *klongs* (canals). You can book a tour at any travel agency, or charter a long-

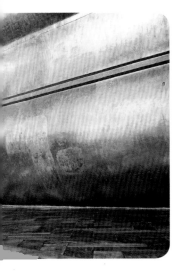

lain and coloured glass, the 67 m/220ft high *prang* of this "Temple of the Dawn" is Thailand's highest Khmer-style tower, a landmark on Bangkok's skyline and a tourist magnet. Despite its popularity, the thousands of small, golden bells are still enchanting, tinkling gently in the breeze while you walk around this narrow site. *Daily 8.30am–5.30pm | admission 50 baht | in Thonburi | boats depart regularly from Tha Thien Pier near Wat Pho over the river*

WAT PHO (U A4) *(ฝ a4)*

The oldest university of the country was founded in 1789 in this temple south of the Grand Palace. The complex accommodates a 46-m (151-ft) long gilded reclining Buddha with mother of pearl inlays on the soles of its feet. Get a relaxing and invigorating ● massage *(from 420 baht per hour),* either in the temple grounds in the often crowded massage pavillon or a few hundred metres beyond at the *Wat Pho massage school (Maharaj Rd | in an alleyway near the pier | tel. 0 26 22 35 51 | www.wat phomassage.com),* the most famous in Thailand. *Daily 8am–6.30pm | admission 100 baht | entrances on Chetuphun, Maharaj and Thai Wang Rd | www.wat pho.com*

tailed motorboat with driver. Boats are available on the Chao Phraya river (behind the Grand Palace at the Tha Chang pier or at the Sathon pier near the Saphan Taksin Skytrain station). *Approx. 1000–1,200 baht per hour (negotiable!)*

INSIDER TIP ▶ MUSEUM OF SIAM ● (U A4) *(ฝ a4)*

Anything but a boring museum. You can feel, listen, see and touch artefacts in this interactive museum. If you are interested in discovering what *Thainess* really is and have always wanted to dress up as a real princess, come here to take the ultimate selfie. The fun multimedia exhibits tell the story of Thailand from the emergence of Siam to the lifestyle of the present day. *Tue–Sun 10am–6pm | admission 200 baht, after 4pm free | Sanamchai Rd*

WAT ARUN ☀ (U A4) *(ฝ a4)*

Truly magical! The "Temple of the Dawn" is one of Bangkok's main landmarks. Richly decorated in multihued porce-

FOOD & DRINK

CABBAGES & CONDOMS ● (U F5) *(ฝ f5)*

Visit this atmospherically illuminated garden restaurant at Christmas time and you'll be greeted by a Santa Claus made entirely out of condoms. The theme of this establishment revolves around love and contraception and the large fantasy figures decorated in coloured condoms are novelty features. Even the bill comes with a condom. This restaurant belongs to an organisation for birth control and

AIDS prevention. *10 Sukhumvit Rd, Soi 12 | tel. 022294610 | Moderate–Expensive*

INSIDER TIP SALA RATTANAKOSIN ☀ (U A4) (*m a4*)

What a view – straight from the Arabian Nights! This elegant hotel restaurant near the Grand Palace serves delightful western-style and Thai dishes. The patio with a view of the river and the Wat Arun when it is lit up at night is very romantic. Reserve early for a table at the window or on the terrace. *39 Maharat Rd | alley behind Wat Pho | tel. 0262213 88 | www.salahospitality. com | Expensive*

INSIDER TIP SEVEN SPOONS (U B3) (*m b3*)

A chic, but restrained atmosphere combined with friendly and competent service plus excellent, Mediterranean-inspired cuisine with an Asian flair at very reasonable prices. The cocktails are tasty, too. *22–24 Chakkrapatipong Rd | tel. 026299214 | www.sevenspoonsbkk. com | Moderate–Expensive*

SIROCCO (U C6) (*m c6*)

This is where your best clothes come into operation: getting all dolled up is a must in one of the highest open air restaurants in the world (220 m/722 ft). Western-style, Mediterranean cuisine and a highlight in every regard: culinary, visually and also in price. Afterwards, enjoy a cocktail at the ● *Sky Bar.* No admittance in shorts, flip-flops, open sandals, sneakers etc. *Daily from 6pm, with reservation only | State Tower | 1055 Silom Rd | tel. 026249555 | www.lebua.com/ sirocco | Expensive*

SHOPPING

The main shopping streets are *Sukhumvit Rd* (U F4–5) (*m f4–5*), *Silom Rd* (U C–D 5–6) (*m c–d 5–6*), *Ploenchit* (U E4) (*m e4*) and first and foremost,

Literally everything can be found on Chatuchak Weekend Market

Rama I Rd (U D–E4) (*m d–e4*) around Siam Skytrain station. There you'll find gigantic shopping centres as well as boutiques and street merchants. At the ultra-posh shopping centre ● *Siam Paragon*, for example, the range of products is staggering: You can get just about everything here, even a brand new Lamborghini. A quite unique area with special shops and plenty of hustle and bustle is Chinatown – walk down *Sampeng Lane* (U B4) (*m b4*) at any time of day.

ASIATIQUE THE RIVERFRONT
(0) (*m 0*)

South of the Taksin Bridge, several old warehouses on the river have been tastefully converted into a huge night-time market. Alongside lots of shops, you can check out the good restaurants, a ☀ ferris wheel *(admission 400 baht)* with a fantastic view and the popular travesty show at *Calypso Cabaret (shows daily 7.30pm and 9pm | 900–1500 baht | tel. 0 26 88 14 15 | www.calypsocabaret.com). Daily from 4pm | 2194 Charoen Krung Rd | www.asiatiquethailand.com*

CHATUCHAK WEEKEND MARKET
★ (0) (*m 0*)

One of the largest markets in the world – not hard to believe once you've been round all 10,000 stalls on more than 86,000 acres – selling a truly mind-boggling array of goods. From guitars to garden implements, t-shirts to teapots, it's all here, and a paradise for those who just love to rummage around – almost half a million people every weekend. *Sat, Sun 6am–6pm | Paholyothin Rd | by the Mo Chit Skytrain station, Chatuchak Park metro station | www.chatuchak.org*

INSIDER TIP SIAM SQUARE
(U D4) (*m d4*)

Just go with the flow: A warren of alleyways with hundreds of shops: clothing, shoes, accessories at every turn. This is also the venue for young Thai designers to showcase their newest creations. The multilevel *Siam Square One (www.siamsquareone.com)* brings hundreds of shops under one roof. *Rama I Rd | across from the Siam Paragon Shopping Centre*

SPORTS & LEISURE

Learn the secrets of Thai cuisine in a cookery course, for example at the noble ● *Blue Elephant (from 3300 baht | 233 Sathorn Tai Rd | tel. 0 26 73 93 53 | www.blueelephantcookingschool.com)* or at the *Baipai Thai Cookery School (2200 baht | course participants are picked up | tel. 0 25 11 14 04 | www.baipai.com)*.

ENTERTAINMENT

INSIDER TIP ABOVE ELEVEN ☀
(0) (*m 0*)

Stylish, modern and yet still cosy rooftop bar on the 33rd floor with a fantastic view of the city, delicious cocktails and snacks. The same applies for the related *Gramercy Park* a floor above. *Daily 6pm–2am | Sukhumvit Rd, Soi 11 | tel. 0 20 38 51 11 | www.aboveeleven.com*

ROUTE 66 (0) (*m 0*)

Live bands and DJs provide the entertainment at this bar where guests dance between the tables. On the table stands the obligatory bottle of whiskey with coke served with plenty of ice, typical in Thailand. This vast club spreads out over three floors (hip-hop, Thai live music, electro) and attracts a young crowd of partygoers. Packed to the rafters on weekends. *Daily 8pm–2am | admission 300 baht | Royal City Av. | tel. 0 22 03 04 07 | www.route66club.com*

INSIDERTIP ARIYASOMVILLA
(U F4) *(𝄞 f4)*

The jungle-like garden with tropical greenery and swimming pool is reason enough to stay in this delightful villa. Located in a central yet tranquil setting, the rooms are individually outfitted with Thai features. There's also a very friendly service, an opulent breakfast and pleasant atmosphere. *24 rooms | 65 Sukhumvit Rd, Soi 1 | tel. 0 22 54 88 80 | www.ariyasom.com | Expensive*

THE ATLANTA (U F4) *(𝄞 f4)*

This legendary 1950s hotel oozes retro charm. You may even suddenly find yourself part of a Thai soap opera since the opulent art déco lobby is often used as a film set. The hotel also has a "zero tolerance" policy to sex tourists, drugs and even cigarettes. Rooms are simple, spacious and clean. Nice garden with Thailand's oldest hotel pool. *59 rooms | 78 Sukhumvit Rd, Soi 2 | tel. 0 22 52 60 69 | www.theatlantahotelbangkok.com | Budget*

BAAN K RESIDENCE (U E5) *(𝄞 e5)*

The spacious, apartment-like rooms offer every comfort and the staff is very helpful. It is worth paying the slightly higher price for the executive rooms. *28 rooms | 12/1 North Sathorn Rd, Soi 2 | tel. 0 26 33 99 11 | www.baankresidence.com | Moderate*

INSIDERTIP BANGKOK LOFT INN
(U A6) *(𝄞 a6)*

This friendly hotel is away from the overcrowded tourist hotspots but still central on the opposite banks of the river. It invites guests to be part of everyday Thai life in the centre of Thonburi. Small extras such as pick-up service, fruit bowl, skytrain day tickets and last, but not least the welcoming atmosphere with travel tips make your stay here really enjoyable. *32 rooms | 55 Somdet Phra Chao Taksin Rd | Thonburi | tel. 0 28 62 04 92 | www.bangkokloftinn.com | Budget*

INSIDERTIP CASA NITHRA
(U B2) *(𝄞 b2)*

Very pleasant and modern boutique hotel for backpackers with higher standards. The bathroom is a true wellness oasis. Terrific view over the old town from the ☀ pool on the roof. *75 rooms | 176 Samsen Rd | tel. 0 26 28 62 28 | www.casanithra.com | Moderate*

BANGKOK TOURISM DIVISION (BTD)
(U A3) *(𝄞 a3)*

BTD info booths can be found everywhere in the city; you can get the best information at the heaquarters. *Mon–Fri 8am–7pm, Sat/Sun 9am–5pm | 17/1 Phra Athit Rd | near the National Theater | tel. 02 2 25 76 12 | www.bangkoktourist.com*

KANCHANA-BURI

(130 C5) *(𝄞 C9)* **You can almost hear "Camera, lights, action!" in this provincial capital. Kanchanaburi (pop. 50,000) attracts foreign visitors in droves who come for the world-famous Bridge over the River Kwai.**

Although the Oscar-prized film with the same name and featuring Alec Guinness was filmed in the Sri Lankan jungle,

Kanchanaburi (situated 130 km/81 miles west of Bangkok) is the site of the actual battlefield. The reconstructed Japanese "death railway" was built in 1942/43 by prisoners of war and thousands of lives were lost in the process. Trains to Kanchanaburi leave Bangkok's Noi Railway Station in the district of Thonburi twice daily at 7.50am and 1.55pm.

SIGHTSEEING

BRIDGE OVER THE RIVER KWAI AND DEATH RAILWAY

Just imagine the horrific jungle conditions during World War II in 1942: The Japanese occupying forces in Thailand have invaded Burma (today Myanmar) and are heading to India. Their plan is to build a 415 km/260 miles long railway line through the tropical jungle. An estimated 60,000 allied prisoners of war and 200,000 forced labourers from Asia slaved on the construction of the "Death Railway" enduring heat, monsoons, landslides, torture and malaria. Many died in the process. Today, thousands of tourists cross the reconstructed *Bridge on the River Kwai* on foot, carrying their colourful parasols to avoid the heat. As soon as the whistling trains are approaching, everyone crowds onto the wooden passing platforms. In fact, only the iron girders are from the original bridge, which stood 4 km/2.5 miles further south and was destroyed by the Allies in 1945.

Try and buy a ticket for the ★ ● *Death Railway (10.55am and 4.26pm | tourist trains that take you over the bridge only 8am–4pm, approx. 30 min. for 150 baht)* that takes you to the final stop on the line. The most spectacular scenery on this railway line starts after the Kwai Bridge as the train winds around sheer cliffs high above the river and crawls over a creaking viaduct near the village of *Wang Po.* The last stop on the line, *Nam Tok* (70 km/42 miles from the bridge), is a sleepy outcrop. If you don't want to return to Kanchanaburi, you can take the bus via the Sai Yok National Park to Sangklaburi.

Not suitable for Hollywood, but world famous: the Bridge over the River Kwai in Kanchanaburi

WAR CEMETERIES AND MUSEUMS

A total of 6,982 Allied prisoners of war are buried at the *Kanchanaburi War Cemetery* between the city and the bridge. On the banks of the Kwai, 2 km/1.2 mile south of the city, is the *Chungkai War Cemetery* with an additional 1,750 graves. You can take a boat from the bridge along the river to get there; tours also take in the *Wat Tham Khao Poon* monastery and its stalactite caves.

Of the three war museums on offer in Kanchanaburi, the *Thailand-Burma Railway Centre (daily 9am–5pm | admission 140 baht | www.tbrconline.com)* across from the Kanchanaburi War Cemetery is the one worth seeing most. The exhibition on the history of the "Death Railway" provides a poignant account of the conditions endured by the POWs forced to build the railway. The older *Jeath War Museum (daily 8.30am–6pm | admission 40 baht | on the site of the Wat Chai Chumpol)* displays letters and photos of the forced labourers in replica bamboo shelters. The *World War II and Jeath War Museum (daily 9am–5pm | admission 40 baht | close to the bridge on the south bank of the river)* houses a curious collection of local artefacts and military equipment.

FOOD & DRINK

INSIDERTIP BLUE RICE RESTAURANT 🍴

The menu is modest, the blue rice just a gag (it's actually stained with pea-flower petals) but the river views while enjoying the gentle breeze make this restaurant irresistible. This peaceful garden restaurant on the other side of the river serves excellent Thai cuisine, explained by chef Noi in a mouthwatering way. (She also runs cooking classes). *153/4 Moo 4 | Thamakham | tel. 0 34 51 20 17 | www.applenoikanchanaburi.com | Budget*

MANGOSTEEN CAFÉ AND BOOKS

Small and cosy café-restaurant with a diverse menu located on the tourist street that dishes up decent portions for a cheap price. A larger branch is located on the other side of the river near the Blue Rice restaurant. *13 Mae Nam Kwae Rd | mobile tel. 08 17 93 58 14 | www.mangosteencafe.net | Budget*

WHERE TO STAY

Book in advance for a weekend stay. Many hotels and raft accommodations are centered on package tours.

BAMBOO HOUSE

The moored house rafts 300 m below the bridge are idyllic, but spartan. More

LOW BUDGET

If you don't want to explore *Old Sukhothai* on foot, hire a motor rickshaw – or a bike, which is cheaper. It's available in many guesthouses and at the park entrance (10–50 baht per day).

In Bangkok most travellers head straight for the guesthouses on the *Khao San Rd* (U A–B3) *(▯ a–b3)*. But even the more costly places on *Sukhumvit Rd* are still reasonable: The modern, friendly *Sleepbox* hostel (U F5) *(▯ f5) (404 Sukhumvit Rd, Soi 22, Soi Sainamthip 3 | tel. 0 26 63 30 88 | sleepbox22.com)* is the perfect base to lay your head. Who needs more when you have the exciting city of Bangkok to explore?

More beautiful than any pool designer could imagine: swimming fun at the Erawan Waterfall

comfortable rooms in terraced houses and a bungalow. Beautiful garden. *19 rooms. | Soi Vietnam | mobile tel. 09 8897 44 02 | Budget*

FELIX RIVER KWAI RESORT
A somewhat faded luxury awaits you right on the river, only 100 m above the bridge. Two pools, sauna, fitness centre, tennis court. *254 rooms | tel. 0 34 55 10 00 | www.felixriverkwai.co.th | Moderate*

INSIDER TIP ORIENTAL KWAI
A true gem awaits 17 km (10.5 miles) northwest of Kanchanaburi with a loving attention to detail such as the bamboo bath, hammocks and tropical river views from the bungalow or the sunlounger at the jetty. Excellently-run and romantic little resort with a pool and a pleasant atmosphere. *12 rooms | 194/5 Moo 1 | La-dya | mobile tel. 06 16 73 0670 | www. orientalkwai.com | Moderate–Expensive*

INFORMATION

TOURISM AUTHORITY OF THAILAND
Information for the entire province is available here. *14 Saeng Chuto Rd | tel. 0 34 51 12 00*

WHERE TO GO

INSIDER TIP ERAWAN WATERFALLS
(130 B5) (*ꞈ B8*)
The waterfalls, located 70 km (43 miles) to the northwest of Kanchanaburi in the 550 sq. km (135,900 acre) *Erawan National Park (daily 8am–4.30pm | admission 300 baht)* are among the most beautiful in the country. Refreshingly cool water cascades over calc-sinter deposits on seven levels. There is a wonderful bathing area at the third level, but it is a sweaty 90 minute walk up to the last of the seven steps. Plan to visit in the morning when it is cooler and less crowded.

SANGKLABURI ★
(130 A4) (*⑪ B7*)

Sangklaburi (pop. 15,000), the last town before the Myanmar border, is 230 km (143 miles) northwest of Kanchanaburi on the shores of the *Khao Laem Reservoir* with the spire of the temple of the flooded old town still visible. Accomodation at *P. Guesthouse (34 rooms | Si Suwan Khiri Rd | tel. 0 34 59 50 61 | www.p-guesthouse.com | Budget)* or with a pool at the *Samprasob Resort (43 rooms | 122 Nongloo | tel. 0 34 59 50 50 | www.samprasob.com | Budget–Moderate)*. A must-see is the unique INSIDER TIP▶ *Wat Wang Wiwekaram* temple complex. The striking multi-tiered roof rises up to the sky and the 60 m/200 ft high, golden pagoda tower is richly decorated with

to Myanmar is currently only open for Thai and Burmese people.

SUKHOTHAI

(127 D6) (*⑪ C5*) **Thousands of lanterns light up the night skies and the rivers are filled with floating, illuminated *Kratong* baskets. The Siamese festival of light, Loi Kratong, held at the end of November, is the highlight of any visit to Sukhothai and brings to life ancient times among its ruins. That said it's worth visiting the royal city at any time.** This is because the "Father of Thailand", King Ram Khamhaeng, is credited not only for the creation of the Thai alphabet (for which the Thais are truly grate-

The Buddha statue in the ruins of Wat Mahathat in Old Sukhothai has aged gracefully

enigmatic signs and symbols – the temple offers a great backdrop for the perfect selfie! On the *Three Pagoda Pass* 30 km/18.5 miles away, set in the bleak mountain environment, is a line of three weather-beaten chedis. The local border

ful) 800 years ago, but for his great achievements in this city: Sukhothai is also the "cradle of the nation" and flourished between the 13th and 14th century. Its architecture and religious art from this period are considered to be the most splendid examples, such as the laughing and striding Buddha, which today stands in the National Museum. Founded in 1238, the old town lies approx. 12 km/7.5 miles from the modern city of Sukhothai (pop. 37,000). This vast Unesco World Heritage Site has over 20 buildings, half of which are well-preserved temple shrines with majestic Buddha statues and a unique, almost mystical, atmosphere especially at sunrise and sunset.

SIGHTSEEING

OLD SUKHOTHAI ★

The biggest and finest temple in Sukhothai is *Wat Mahathat* with the main chedi standing on a pedestal and numerous Buddha statues, some of which have been restored. Nearby are the three prangs of *Wat Si Sawai*, while after walking through the *San Luang gate,* to the north of the formerly walled city centre, the chedi at *Wat Phra Phai Luang*, one of the oldest monastery sites in Sukhothai (800 years old) stands on an island in an artificial pool. Next to that is *Wat Sri Chum*, famous for its enormous seated Buddha (11 m/36 ft high – the largest in Sukhothai) contained within the walls and wooden leaf doors. The temples at the park can be explored by bicycle, for example on an informative guided mountain bike tour with *Cycling Sukhothai (approx. 1000 baht | mobile tel. 08 50 83 18 64 | www.cycling-sukhothai. com)*, who also offer tours around the countryside. *Daily 6.30am–6.30pm | admission 100 baht per zone (centre, north and west),* ● *Sun–Fri from 6pm admission free in the central zone*

RAMKHAMHAENG NATIONAL MUSEUM

Meeting a Buddha is a special experience in itself – but at this museum you come face to face with one of the most iconic Sukhothai works of art, the magnificent striding Buddha. There are only a handful of these statues left in Thailand. One copy stands at the central old town site of Wat Sra Sri. The collection contains many more Buddha figures and other exhibits from the Sukhothai period. *Daily 9am–4pm | admission 150 baht | at the park entrance*

FOOD & DRINK

Enjoy Thai food at the *night market on Ramkhamhaeng Rd* in New Sukhothai, for example at the popular INSIDER TIP *Rom Pho*. Simple food stalls directly at the park entrance serve local and Western dishes.

WHERE TO STAY

THE LEGENDHA SUKHOTHAI

This charming resort approx. 1.5 km/1 mile from the entrance to the Historic Park, uses a lot of wood and classic Thai design. Rooms with all conveniences, pool. *55 rooms | 214 Jarodvithi Thong Rd | tel. 0 55 69 72 14 | www.legendhasukhothai.com | Moderate–Expensive*

RUEAN THAI HOTEL

The former guesthouse is now called a hotel, but it has remained a stylish small place to stay, with lovely, comfortable rooms and a pool in the courtyard. *27 rooms | 181/20 Jarodvithi Thong Rd, Soi Pracharuammit | tel. 0 55 61 24 44 | www.rueanthaihotel.com | Budget–Expensive*

INFORMATION

TOURISM AUTHORITY OF THAILAND

200 Jarodvithi Thong Rd | opposite the Shell service station | New Sukhothai | tel. 0 55 61 62 28

THE NORTH

Any trip to Thailand would certainly not be complete without visiting the north of the country.

Roads run up and down the last foothills of the Himalayas like rollercoasters with amazing photo opportunities on virtually every hairpin bend in the road. The Burmese-Laotian wooden temples are amazing to see as are the brightly coloured traditional costumes worn by the hill tribes. Tourists who are pushed for time have to make a difficult decision of what to do: From trekking to the hill tribes to concocting dishes with explosively hot ingredients in a cooking course, there are thousands of things to do and see. Free your itinerary so that you can spend a few exciting days exploring Thailand's north!

CHIANG MAI

(126 C3) (ℳ B3) The region's largest city, with a population of 200,000, is situated in the fertile valley of the Ping River.

Founded in 1296, it was the capital city of the kingdom of Lanna until 1558. Today, the metropolis of the north impresses with more than 100 monasteries. But don't stress yourself: it's sufficient to see only the most picturesque ones.

SIGHTSEEING

OLD TOWN ★

Behind the moat and the partially preserved brick city wall, the Old Town has

Photo: Wat Phra That Doi Kong Mu in Mae Hong Son

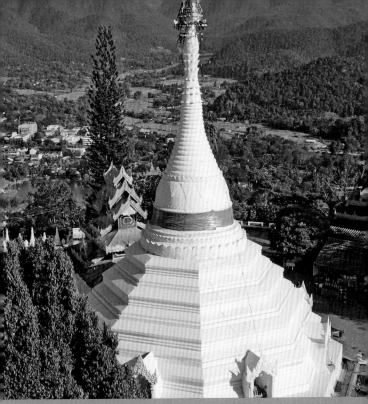

Adventure and culture: take a walk through the temple city of Chiang Mai and discover the land of the hill tribes

CITY WHERE TO START?
Tapae Gate: This gate takes you to the Ratchadamnoen Rd which leads straight to historic Chiang Mai. In the opposite direction Tapae Rd leads to the commercial centre of the town. Both areas can be easily explored on foot. If you're not staying in the town centre, let a Tuk-Tuk chauffeur you there.

managed to retain much of its charm. You will encounter a delightful temple every few minutes; admission is not free everywhere anymore. But there are still some free oases among the lesser visited sites, such as ● *Wat Chiang Man (Ratchapakinat Rd)* which is well worth seeing because of its exquisite carvings, wall paintings, elephant sculptures at the foot of the chedi as well as two small, but legendary Buddha statues. If you only want to visit one single temple in Chiang Mai, it has got to be this

No visit to the north would be complete without visiting the Wat Chedi Luang Temple in Chiang Mai

one: The once 86-m (282-ft) high chedi of *Wat Chedi Luang (Phrappoklao Rd | daily approx. 6.30am–5pm | admission 40 baht)* was partially destroyed by an earthquake in 1545, yet it is still an imposing sight at half that height, a restored 42 m/140 ft, and it even looks a little like from an Indiana Jones movie – especially in the late afternoon when you're almost alone there. Very popular: the *Monk Chat (daily 9am–6pm)* with the monks. Another gem is *Wat Phra Sing (Sam Lan/Sigharat Rd)* with its unique library building, a masterpiece of timber construction from the Lanna era.

Three museums await visitors around the Sam Kasat Monument. The interesting *Chiang Mai City Arts & Cultural Centre,* the the less worthwhile *Chiang Mai Historical Centre* and the *Lanna Folklife Museum* (small, but interesting because of its life-size figures) provide background information on local history, culture and art. *Tue–Sun 8.30am–5pm | admission each 90 baht, joint ticket 180 baht | Phra Pokklao Rd | www.cmocity. com*

FOOD & DRINK

There are food stands at the *Galare Food Center* across from the night market, as well as opposite the Chang Puak Gate in the north of the Old Town.

AROON RAI

Don't be deterred by the canteen atmosphere with plastic chairs and open tin pots. If you are looking to try the classic northern Thai curry noodle soup **INSIDER TIP** *khao soi*, Aroon Rai is the place to go. This simple open restaurant has been serving inexpensive Thai cuisine for over 50 years. *45 Kotchasan Rd | tel. 0 53 27 69 47 | Budget*

LA FONTANA

Tasty pizzas and pasta are prepared in this authentic and inviting Italian restaurant at a good price. *Ratchamanka Rd 39/7–8 | tel. 0 53 20 70 91 | www.lafonta nachiangmai.com | Budget–Moderate*

THE RIVERSIDE

Evenings feature really good live music at this terraced restaurant on the Ping River. As a novelty, order off the menu aboard the excursion boat *(75-minute river journey daily at 8pm)*. *9–11 Charoen Rat Rd | tel. 0 53 24 32 39 | www.theriversidechiang mai.com | Budget–Moderate*

SHOPPING

Handicrafts and needlework produced by the hill tribes are abundant, especially at the *night market (Night Bazaar | Chang Klan Rd* and at *Tapae Gate.* The street from the gate into the Old Town is closed to traffic on Sundays to make way for a vast market. Every Saturday, Wualai Road south of the old town is turning into *Saturday Walking Street.* The village of *Bor Sang,* east of Chiang Mai, is famous for its colourfully painted paper umbrellas. *Sankampaeng Rd,* leading there, is lined on both sides with shops offering an array of crafts and souvenirs.

SPORTS & LEISURE

Different elephant camps around Chiang Mai offer guided tours. A recommendable option is *Elephant Special Tours (Mae Sopok | Aumpher Mae Wang | mobile tel. 08 61 93 03 77 | www. elephant-tours.de/en)*. Animal keeper Bodo Förster and his mahouts teach you how to steer these grey giants through the jungle and look them in the eye – a one-of-a-kind experience, and for some, a life's dream. A two-day package including room and board starts at around 9000 baht.

ENTERTAINMENT

There are small bar districts in the upper *Loi Kro Rd* near the Old Town and around the *Zoe in Yellow* in *Ratchawithi Rd.* Local students prefer the bars and clubs along the *Nimmanhaemin Rd* (in the northwestern part of town), e.g. *Monkey Club* and *Warm Up.*

WHERE TO STAY

THE 3 SIS

Delightful lodge in the Old Town. All rooms are comfortable, equipped with refrigerators and TVs and done out in typical north Thai Lanna style. *24 rooms | 1 Phrapoklao Rd, Soi 8 | tel. 0 53 27 32 43 | www.the3sis.com | Moderate*

INSIDER TIP ▶ BAAN HANIBAH B & B
Stylish and tastefully decorated rooms are rented out in this old Lanna house made of teak, complete with charmingly creaking floorbards. You will feel at home right away. Other plus factors: the

---

MARCO POLO HIGHLIGHTS

⭐ **The Old Town of Chiang Mai**
Masterpieces of temple construction behind ancient walls
→ p. 46

⭐ **Doi Inthanon**
Take a walk on top of Thailand's highest mountain → p. 50

⭐ **Mae Hong Son**
The temples in this small town will surprise you → p. 52

⭐ **Pai**
The small town attracts seasoned travellers with its alternative vibe → p. 54

quiet location in the Old Town as well as the lovely garden and the friendly staff. *12 rooms | 6 Moon Muang Rd, Soi 8 | tel. 053 28 75 24 | www.baanhanibah.com | Budget*

INSIDER TIP ▶ RACHAMANKHA

Welcome to Nirvana! Reminiscent of a temple complex in the Lanna style, furnished with antiques – the stylish boutique hotel is an oasis of peace with a large pool near Wat Phra Sing.

WHERE TO GO

DOI INTHANON ★ ☀️
(126 B3–4) (*Ø B4*)

For all those aiming high it's up to the summit of Thailand's highest mountain (2,565 m/8,415 ft). In the national park of the same name it's possible to take excursions to waterfalls and to see a hill tribe village. There is a temple near the top; a short nature trail leads through the fairy-tale cloud forest. There are some beautiful

Wat Phra That Doi Suthep, one of the most famous monasteries in Thailand, is a good 700 years old

The rooms are tastefully simple, but elegantly furnished. *24 rooms | 6 Rachamankha Rd | tel. 053 90 41 11 | www.rachamankha.com | Expensive*

INFORMATION

CHIANG MAI MUNICIPAL TOURIST OFFICE
Tapae Rd | tel. 053 25 25 57

vistas as you drive up the mountain and it is interesting to observe the changing climatic zones within such a short space of time. Don't forget to take a jacket or pullover! *Admission 300 baht, tours from Chiang Mai from 1400 baht | 100 km (60 miles) southwest of Chiang Mai*

WAT PHRA THAT DOI SUTHEP ☀️
(126 C3) (*Ø B3*)

This monastery on Mt Suthep (1,676 m/5,499 ft) is famous throughout Thailand. It is located at a height of 1,070 m (3,510 ft) and was built in 1338 as a repository for a Buddha relic. From the car park, a staircase with 306 steps flanked by mythical Naga serpent leads up there. If you're not up to that, there's always the funicular. *Daily 8am–5pm | admission 30 baht, with funicular 50 baht, tour approx. 550 baht | public minibuses (50 baht) from Chang Puak Bus Station (500 m north of Chang Puak Gate) run daily until 3pm as a shuttle service | 16 km (10 miles) northwest of Chiang Mai*

CHIANG RAI

(127 D2) *(ഝ C2)* **Chiang Rai, capital of the province of the same name, was founded in 1262.**

The city of 67, 000 inhabitants is the economic hub of the far north, but it is much quieter than Chiang Mai.

SIGHTSEEING

HILLTRIBE MUSEUM

The Hilltribe Museum provides information on the culture of six tribal groups in northern Thailand, and organises ⊗ socially compatible trekking tours. *Mon–Fri 9am–6pm, Sat/Sun 10am–6pm | admission 50 baht | Tanalai Rd | tel. 053 74 00 88 | www.pdacr.org*

INSIDER TIP ▶ **WAT RONG KHUN**

Buddha meets Batman in this surreal temple complex created by a famous Thai artist. Clad entirely in white, this masterpiece of architecture, sculptures and paintings is like no other temple in Thailand, especially regarding its kitsch factor. *Daily approx. 8am–5.30pm | admission 50 baht | 13 km/8 miles south on Hwy. 1*

FOOD & DRINK/ SHOPPING

You'll find a large selection of food stalls at the *night market* in the city centre. It is not as large as the one in Chiang Mai, but the handicrafts and other products made by the hill tribe artisans cost rather less. Folklore dances are also staged here.

WHERE TO STAY

KANLAYA PLACE

Centrally-located, inexpensive and friendly accommodation with clean rooms. The rooms facing the street can be a bit loud due to the bars outside. *9 rooms | tel. 053 60 17 56 | 428/5 Jetyod Rd, Soi 8 | Budget*

THE LEGEND CHIANG RAI BOUTIQUE RIVER RESORT

Enjoy a dose of luxury in the northeast of the city thanks to your elegant and very spacious room plus the riverside infinity pool. *78 rooms | Moo 21 | 124/15 Kohloy Rd | tel. 053 91 04 00 | www.thelegend-chiangrai.com | Expensive*

INFORMATION

TOURISM AUTHORITY OF THAILAND
448/16 Singhaklai Rd | tel. 053 74 46 74

WHERE TO GO

INSIDER TIP **MAE SALONG** ✲
(127 D1) *(ഝ C2)*

This village (also called Santi Khiri, 67 km/41.5 miles northwest of Chiang Rai) on the 1,355-m/4,445-ft high Doi Mae Salong is inhabited by descendants of Chinese Kuomintang soldiers, who fled to Thailand through Burma (now Myanmar) after Mao Zedong's Revolution.

They grow tea, coffee and vegetables. Teas and dried fruit from China are sold at the market which is also frequented by members of the various hill tribes. The *Chinese Martyr's Museum* is located at the entrance to the village. A comfortable place to stay with a fantastic view of the village is ☆ *Baan See See Mountain View (24 rooms | tel. 0 53 76 50 53 | Budget).*

SOP RUAK (127 D1) (*C2*)

Once a notorious hideout for smugglers, the playing grounds for vicious wars between drug lords and famous for its endless fields of red poppies, Sop Ruak now claims name and fame for the point where three countries – Laos, Myanmar and Thailand meet. Today, the so-called centre of the famous Golden Triangle is a purely tourist attraction and the drug traffickers have now been replaced by buses full of tourists. The little village of Sop Ruak is packed with souvenir stalls. You can track down the infamous drug lords in one of the country's best museums: The enormous **INSIDER TIP** *Hall of Opium (Tue–Sun 10am–5pm, last admission 4pm | admission 200 baht | www. maefahluang.org)* features multimedia and interactive exhibitions which include a fascinating insight into the drug trade of the past and today and its effects. Even opium poppy still grows here – albeit behind glass. *70 km (43 miles) north of Chiang Rai*

MAE HONG SON

(126 B2) (*A3*) **If you think one temple in Thailand looks pretty much like another, then think again! The tranquil town of ★ Mae Hong Son has several gems, all built in typical Burmese gingerbread style – with plenty of wood, gold and lots of frills.**

Near the Myanmar border and surrounded by mountains, the smallest provincial capital in the country (pop. 20,000) once

Two Lisu girls in Mae Salong wearing the colourful costumes of their hill tribe

earned the sobriquet "The Siberia of Thailand". Today, even planes land here. The environs are perfect for those who like to go exploring off the beaten track.

SIGHTSEEING

On the picturesque *Chong Kam Lake* in the middle of the town are ● the filigree temples of *Wat Chong Klang* and *Wat Chong Kham (free admission to both)*. It is particularly romantic here when mist hangs over the lake in the early morning. There are breathtaking views from the monastery on the 424-m (1391-ft) high ☀ *Doi Kong Mu*.

FOOD & DRINK

Food stalls are situated at the *night market* on the lake. Thai cuisine accompanied by live music can be found at the *Sunflower Café (Moderate)*; for good pizza try *Primavera (Budget–Moderatte)* in the south of the city centre on the main road.

FERN RESTAURANT

This large restaurant is a local classic. Behind its pretty wooden façade, it serves a mixture of exotic dishes such as fried fern and local specialties. The Thai dishes have a Burmese touch using the traditional cooking skills of the Burmese Shan. *87 Khunlumpraphat Rd | tel. 0 53 61 13 74 | Budget–Moderate*

WHERE TO STAY

B2 MAE HONG SON PREMIER RESORT

Located on the northern edge of the town, this boutique hotel belongs to a new generation of hotels with its trendy design, large bright rooms with all amenities and a delightful pool. At the time of going to print, the hotel did not have its own restaurant. However, it is only ten minutes on foot to the centre where you can eat breakfast. *42 rooms | 11 Sirimongkol Rd | tel. 0 53 24 28 38 | www. b2hotel.com | Budget*

INSIDER TIP FERN RESORT ☺

Set among rice paddies, this hotel couldn't have a greener setting. It may show signs of ageing but this award-winning ecological resort is nestled among nature. Comfortable, climatised wooden bungalows, pool. The staff all come from the area. Only the freshest ingredients purchased at local markets are used in the kitchen. *36 rooms | Pha Bong | 9 km/5 miles outside the city | tel. 0 53 68 61 10 | www.fernresort.info | Moderate*

INFORMATION

TOURISM AUTHORITY OF THAILAND
4 Rajthampitak Rd | tel. 0 53 61 29 82

LOW BUDGET

For only 350 baht per person or 2200 baht boat charter you can speed down the Kok River from Thaton to Chiang Rai – in a roofed motor boat *(daily around 10.30am from Chiang Rai, 12.30pm from Thaton, duration 3–4 hrs)*. But this trip is not very comfortable!

Nowhere in Thailand can you delve into the delights of Thai cuisine as cheaply as in Chiang Mai. Prices for a day cooking class start at 1500 baht, for example at the ☺ *Thai Farm Cooking School (Moon Muang Rd, Soi 9 | mobile tel. 08 12 88 59 89 | www. thaifarmcooking.net)* on an organic farm.

PAI

MAE AW (126 B2) (*m A2*)

The trip though wild and remote ☀ mountain landscape to the photogenic Kuomintang village of Mae Aw by a small photogenic reservoir is almost like a journey to the end of the earth. Opium was previously planted here, the inhabitants now live off tourism and their tea plantations. Savour freshly brewed tea and specialities of the Chinese Yunnan cuisine in the small restaurants. The village is officially called

(126 B2) (*m B3*) **However much the small town of** ⭐ **Pai tried to conceal itself behind the high mountains and endless curves and hairpin bends, it couldn't stay hidden forever. Today, this fast growing traveller's paradise in the country's high north has become a hotspot for visitors from around the world.** Its popularity started long before the cinema blockbuster "Pai in Love" hit Thai screens in 2009 and saw a boom

The people of Mae Aw cultivate tea in an idyllic setting - and serve it to their guests

Ban Rak Thai, "the village that loves Thailand".

On your way there, it's worth taking a detour to the INSIDER TIP *Pha Sua National Park (daily 8am–6pm | admission 200 baht | approx. 30 km/18 miles north of Mae Hong Son on road 1095)* for the stunning waterfall with the same name. And if you're lucky, you may encounter a group of wild gibbons along the way.

in local tourists. The hippies were the first to arrive in the 1990s, followed by a wave of backpackers and finally young, hip Thais from Bangkok found their way here. Small Cessna planes arriving from Chiang Mai have been landing here ever since; many tourists no longer have the time for the long and winding road up to Pai with its 762 bends. This once sleepy village with a population of 6000 now resembles a trendy hotspot for rafting and raving, relaxing and trekking, massage and meditation. Souvenirs are available on every corner as well as tattoo parlours, reiki and Thai cooking schools as well as bars and pubs. Boutique hotels and guesthouses now appear to outnumber cheap huts and sleeping dormitories. The *Tha Pai Hot Springs (admission 300 baht | 8 km/5 miles south of Pai)* is the perfect place to relax. You can also bathe in the small waterfalls of *Mo Paeng* and *Pa Bong (8 km/4 miles and 12 km/7 miles northwest of Pai)*.

SIGHTSEEING

INSIDER TIP BAMBOO BRIDGE 🌿

A simple path made of bamboo mats winds through the paddy fields, which are bright green during the rainy season and golden just before the harvest. The 800 m/874 yrd long Kho Ku So (Sacrifice Bridge) was used as a shortcut by the monks from the remote Wat Huay Kai Kiri to the villages where they went collecting charity. There is now a café open for visitors. *Ban Pam Bok | northwest of Pai*

WAT PHRA THAT MAE YEN 🌿

You have 335 steps to climb before you can enjoy the splendid panorama from the temple. The view is particular beautiful in November and December when the *thale mok,* the "sea of mist", hovers over the valley. *2 km/1.2 mile outside Pai near the village of Mae Yen*

FOOD & DRINK

There's good Thai food at *Na's Kitchen (Budget)* near the school and the traditional *Baan Benjarong (Budget–Moderate)* on the town's edge in the direction of Chiang Mai. Recommended: the organic cuisine at the ☯ *Good Life Restaurant (Budget)* as well as in the popular *Om's Garden Café (Budget)*.

ENTERTAINMENT

Many bars in Pai are fly-by-night, but there is always a party somewhere. The *Jiko Bar* right in the centre is equally popular with locals and tourists.

WHERE TO STAY

REVERIE SIAM RESORT

If you want to splurge a bit, this is just the right place. Luxury rooms decorated in colonial style with antiques, a chic retro villa, two pools, very accommodating staff and an excellent restaurant. *20 rooms | 476 Moo 8 | Vieng Tai | tel. 0 53 69 98 70 | www.reveriesiam.com | Expensive*

RIM PAI COTTAGE

Rustic, comfortable wooden bungalows on a nice site right on the river near the town centre. *20 rooms | tel. 0 53 69 91 33 | www.rimpaicottage.com | Moderate*

WHERE TO GO

SOPPONG (126 B2) (*Ω A–B 2–3*)

Around the small, wild market town 43 km/27 miles west of Pai, there are several giant, largely unexplored caves. Take a few hours for an adventurous tour through the *Mae Lanna Cave (from 750 baht per person)* or cross the 500 m long (546 yd) stalactite cave *Tham Lot* 8 km (5 miles) north of Soppong on a bamboo raft *(450 baht incl. guide for up to 3 people)*. Ask at the local hotels for more information about the tours: the rustic bungalows at the *Cave Lodge (tel. 0 53 61 72 03 | www.cavelodge.com | Budget)* are nearby. A more comfortable place in the village itself is *Little Eden Guesthouse (mobile tel. 08 99 52 88 70 | www.littleeden-guesthouse.com | Budget–Moderate)*.

THE NORTHEAST

The northeast offers a different, surprising side to Thailand with its flat, dry and barren ground. Isan is home to the country's rice growers and its high plateau stretches to the banks of the Mekong which borders on the neighbouring country of Laos. The vast region covers one third of the country. Those who believe there is nothing to see here are mistaken.

The World Heritage Site, Ban Chiang, is the excavation site of the oldest bronze artefacts of Southeast Asia. Built a few thousands of years later, yet no less impressive, are the most splendid Khmer temples outside Cambodia in Phimai. However, the Isan region offers far more than just ancient remains. The last herds of wild elephants in Thailand roam the

Khao Yai National Park. And the best about the northeast: Far away from the familiar tramping grounds of millions of tourists to Thailand, you can discover here authentic traditions, the generosity and hospitality of the Thai people as well as the hot and spicy cuisine.

KHON KAEN

(132 B2) *(ⓜ F6)* **Khon Kaen (pop. 150,000) lies at the heart of Isan, about 450 km (280 miles) from Bangkok.**
Few tourists stop at this university city. Aside from the national museum and temples, the city itself has few noteworthy attractions; there are some interesting destinations in the surrounding area.

Where Thailand has retained its origins:
in the land of rice farmers, on the trail of wild
elephants and ancient cultures

SIGHTSEEING

BUNG KAEN NAKHON

This lake at the southeastern edge of the centre is a popular picnic area. By the lake is the enormous pyramid of INSIDER TIP *Wat Nong Waeng* with exquisitely carved details on doors and shutters.

NATIONAL MUSEUM

An extensive collection of archaeological artefacts including stone and bronze axes from Ban Chiang (see p. 63), a graceful bronze Buddha from the Sukhothai period and a Shiva statue from the 11th century. *Wed–Sun 9am–4pm | admission 100 baht | Langsunratchakan Rd*

FOOD & DRINK

You can sample the wide range of typical Isan fare for a few pounds at the ● *night market*. Good Western food can be had at *Didine Restaurant (7/9 Pracha Samran Rd | Budget–Moderate)*.

ENTERTAINMENT

The central *Pracha Samran Road* has earned the nickname "Disco Street" thanks to its rather wild bar and dancing scene. Popular: the *Rad (no. 231/2)*.

namese), a sushi bar and a karaoke bar. Kronen beer is brewed on the premises. *293 rooms | 9 Prachasumran Rd | tel. 043 322155 | www.pullman khonkaen.com | Moderate–Expensive*

A cobra is the star of the show in the village of Ban Khoksanga

WHERE TO STAY

KOSA HOTEL
The long-established city hotel is reasonably priced and has comfortable rooms. The facility is not the newest, but the rooms are in top form. *194 rooms | 250–252 Srichan Rd | tel. 043 320320 | www.kosahotel.com | Budget–Moderate*

INSIDER TIP PULLMAN KHON KAEN RAJA ORCHID
This is the best hotel in the city, offering five-star luxury in very comfortable rooms at bargain prices. The hotel has a pool and spa, five restaurants (Chinese, Italian, German, Thai, Viet-

INFORMATION

TOURISM AUTHORITY OF THAILAND
15/5 Prachasamoson Rd | tel. 043 244498

WHERE TO GO

Tours to Khon Laen's surroundings can be difficult using public transport. Rent a vehicle instead (with or without a driver, from approx. 1,200 baht) at *Current Service (tel. 043 243545)*.

PHU WIANG NATIONAL PARK
(132 A1) *(Ø F6)*
This park has been dubbed "Dinosaurland". The life-size dinosaur models are

recent, but the fossilised remains of the prehistoric beasts are 120–150 million years old. Follow the trails to the various digs, and study the fossil remains and information panels at the small Visitor Centre. *Admission 200 baht | 85 km (53 miles) northwest of Khon Kaen*

UBONRAT DAM AND COBRA VILLAGE
(132 B1) (*Ⓜ F6*)

The 800-m (0.5-mile) long *Ubonrat dam*, 50 km (31 miles) northwest of Khon Kaen, has created a 410 sq km (158 sq mile) reservoir – a favourite excursion destination with boat trips and a golf course. In the village of *Ban Khok Sa-nga* the *King Cobra Club* presents snakes in enclosures. Villagers step into the ring to pit themselves against the pythons and cobras. It's showtime as long as there are enough spectators; should you be the only visitor, negotiate a price in advance.

NAKHON RATCHASIMA

(132 A4) (*Ⓜ F7–8*) **Commonly known as Korat, the provincial metropolis of Nakhon Ratchasima is the largest city in the northeast with a population of 250,000.**

It is also the gateway to the province of Nakhon Ratchasima. The most interesting sights are to be found in the vicinity.

SIGHTSEEING

MAHA WIRAWONG NATIONAL MUSEUM

This museum's collection contains many Buddha figures, ceramics, carvings and examples of Khmer art. *Wed–Sun 9am–4pm | admission 20 baht | Ratchadamnoen Rd | at Wat Suthachinda*

THAO-SURANARI MEMORIAL

Standing on top of her plinth, the bronze statue commemorates the brave wife of one of Korat's former governors. In 1826, Thao Suranari led the resistance against Laotian invaders and drove them out of the city. Also known as Khun Ying Mo, she is venerated as a saint by the people of Isan, and pilgrims come here every day to light incense sticks and place their offerings. *In the city centre between Ratchadamnoen Rd and Chumphon Rd*

FOOD & DRINK

You will find food stalls at the *night market (Mahattai Rd/corner of Manat Rd)*; good local cuisine is served in the stylish Thai beer garden at the *Ampawa Restaurant (264 Yommarat Rd | Budget–Moderate)* or, more cheaply, at *Happyland (280 Mahattai Rd | Budget)* with noisy live music. At *Chez Andy (closed Sun | 5 Manat Rd | tel. 0 44 28 95 56 | www. chezandykorat.com | Budget–Moderate)*

★ **Khao Yai National Park**
With a bit of luck you'll see wild elephants on your trek, certainly a beautiful jungle world → p. 60

★ **Phimai**
Thailand's most exquisite Khmer temples and ancient banyan trees → p. 61

★ **Ban Chiang National Museum**
Early bronze pieces and beautifully decorated ceramics from one of the oldest settlements in Southeast Asia → p. 63

you can order a proper steak, sausages and hash browns – something hearty for a change.

WHERE TO STAY

DUSIT PRINCESS

The Princess is no longer in her prime, but is still the best hotel in the city. Spacious rooms with modern conveniences and a large pool. *186 rooms | 1137 Suranarai Rd | tel. 0 44 25 66 29 | www. dusit.com | Moderate*

ROMYEN GARDEN PLACE

A large apartment block with fully equipped modern rooms outfitted with kitchenettes. *70 rooms | 168/9 Chomsurangyat Rd | tel. 0 44 26 01 16 | romyengardenplace.com | Budget–Moderate*

LOW BUDGET

Air conditioning, fridge, TV, DVD player, pool: In Nong Khai you'll find such accommodation from 535 baht at the centrally located *Pantawee Hotel (120 Rooms | 1049 Haisoke Rd | tel. 0 42 411 5 68 | www.thailand.pantawee.com)*.

Bobby's Apartment & Jungle Tours (24 rooms | 291 Mittapab Rd | tel. 0 44 32 81 77 | www.bobbysjungletourkhaoyai.com) in Pak Chong takes you cheaply to the Khao-Yai National Park. Day trips with experienced guides cost 1300 baht including admission. You stay in simple but spacious and very affordable rooms and are treated to good and generous meals.

INFORMATION

TOURISM AUTHORITY OF THAILAND
Mittraphap Rd | on the bypass road at the edge of the city, near Hotel Sima Thani | tel. 0 44 21 36 66

WHERE TO GO

You can hire a car with driver, for example from *Korat Car Rental (136 Phonsaen Rd | tel. 0 44 39 37 30 | www.koratcarrental.com)*.

SILK WEAVING VILLAGE
(132 A4) (𝙼 E8)
The village of *Pak Thong Chai* is a major centre of Thai silk production, and you can watch how silk fabrics are woven by hand or produced with modern machinery. Dozens of companies ranging from small family businesses to high-tech manufacturers produce the precious material. If you buy your silk here you can be sure that it's absolutely pure. *32 km (20 miles) southwest | shuttle bus service*

KHAO YAI NATIONAL PARK ★
(131 E–F5) (𝙼 E8)
The oldest national park in the country – and one of the most beautiful – is also the largest elephant reserve. There are still around 300 elephants roaming in herds through the jungle here – which, together with the adjacent sanctuaries of the Dong Phayayen Mountains, is a Unesco World Heritage Site. You'll need a bit of luck to see them, though, and it's advisable to take a guide. There is a better chance that wild boars will cross your path or that hornbills will be flying overhead.

From the *Park Headquarters (mobile tel. 08 60 92 65 29)* you can follow marked jungle trails without a guide, and stop at refreshing waterfalls on the way. You can also hire mountain bikes at the Park Headquarters. Organised tours to the park can be booked at many travel agencies. If you're on your own it's best to approach via *Pak Chong* (87 km/54 miles southwest of Korat) on Highway 2; from there it is a further 35 km (22 miles) to the park. There's also a pick-up service from Pak Chong. There are a number of resorts along the access road and around

seum (Wed–Sun 9am–4pm | admission 100 baht) filled with art and archaeological exhibits from the Isan region. And you can admire some of nature's wonders: the *banyan trees (Sai Ngam)* at the Mun River (1.5 km/1 mile to the east) are several hundred years old.

You'll find accommodation near the park at the modest *Boonsiri Guesthouse (13 rooms | Chomsudasadet Rd | tel. 0 44 47 11 59 | www.boonsiri.net | Budget)*

A moment to hold your breath: Wild elephants in the Khao Yai National Park

the park, and these also offer tours. *Admission 400 baht*

PHIMAI ★ (132 B3) (*ØD F7*)

This small town 58 km (36 miles) northeast of Korat is home to the largest Khmer temple complex outside Cambodia. At the *Phimai Historical Park (daily 7.30am–6pm | admission 100 baht)* imposing sandstone buildings surround the 92-ft-high central prang. Another worthwhile attraction is the *Phimai National Mu-*

with a pretty courtyard. They also organise tours, for example to the ruins of the Khmer temple in *Phanom Rung Historical Park*. Likewise centrally located but more comfortable and even with a pool is the *Pimai Paradise Hotel (42 rooms | 100 Samairuchi Rd | tel. 0 44 28 75 65 | www. phimaiparadisehotel.com | Budget)*.

SURIN (132 C4) (*ØD G8*)

On the third weekend in November, this town of 40,000 inhabitants, capital of

A mythical world of rock at the sculpture park Sala Kaew Ku

the province of the same name, is full of tourists here for the *Elephant Round-Up,* when more than 300 elephants show off their skills. Travel agencies in Bangkok organise special excursions. In the village of *Ta Klang,* 60 km (37 miles) north of Surin is the *Surin Elephant Study Center* that cares for 200 elephants and runs a museum about them. Volunteers are always welcome at the *Surin Project (13,000 baht per week | www.surinproject.org)* working, as does the Study Center, under the roof of the renowned Save Elephant Foundation *(www.saveelephant.org/surin-project).*

Accommodation options in Surin include the hostel *Pirom & Aree's House (9 rooms | 55 Thungpo Rd 326, Soi Arunee | tel. 0 44 51 5140 | Budget)* which is surrounded by a lovely garden; Pirom, a retired social worker, organises tours. Good, affordable local and Western food is served at the no-frills *Starbeam Restaurant (32/6 Soi Saboran 2 | Budget). 170 km (105 miles) east of Korat | arrival by bus or train*

NONG KHAI

(128 C4) *(ØØ F4)* **The provincial capital of Nong Khai (pop. 70,000), a stone's throw from Laos and a good springboard for going there, promises a relaxing stay by the banks of the Mekong.**

The 1.7-km (1 mile) long *Thai-Laos Friendship Bridge* takes you to Vientiane, 26 km (16 miles) away. Trains run over the bridge, but the route to Vientiane is not completed yet.

SIGHTSEEING

INSIDER TIP ▶ SALA KAEW KU (WAT KHAEK)

This temple complex, with its bizarre sculpture garden, is quite unique. Visitors are dwarfed by an astonishing collection of giant Buddha statues, demons, Hindu gods and goddesses, seven-headed cobras, elephants and more. *3 km (2 miles) east*

FOOD & DRINK

In the *German Bakery (Koaworavut Rd | tel. 0 42 41 30 72)* you can get a hearty breakfast and delicious sweet rolls. At ☆ *Mut Mee Garden* belonging to the *Guesthouse* of the same time you can relax and enjoy the river panorama. The *Nagarina* floating restaurant *(www. nagarina.com | Budget)* casts off from below the Guesthouse everyday around 5pm for a INSIDER TIP Sunset Cruise where Laos and Thailand seem to melt into each other in the golden evening light. Food stalls open up in the evenings along *Prajak Rd* opposite the Wat Sri Saket.

SHOPPING

The very crowded *Indochina Market* on the river is chock-full of wares from Laos and China.

VILLAGE WEAVER HANDICRAFTS ◎

There is a large selection of high-quality hand-woven fabrics and clothing at this self-help business project, at fair prices for the producers. *1151 Prachak Rd, Soi Chittanpanya*

WHERE TO STAY

There are several simple, friendly guest-houses on Rimkong Road (along the river), such as the *Ruan Thai Guest House (20 rooms | tel. 0 42 41 25 19 | Budget)*.

INSIDER TIP MUT MEE GUESTHOUSE ☆

Simple bungalows and rooms (not all have air-condition) at this little, friendly oasis right on the river – with a view into Laos! There are many activities on offer; you can, for example, enrol in yoga classes or rent a bicycle here. *36 rooms |*

111/4 Kaeworawut Rd | tel. 0 42 46 07 17 | www.mutmee.com | Budget

ROYAL NAKHARA HOTEL

If you are looking for a dose of comfort, this hotel is the best in town. At Royal Nakhara Hotel, you can relax in spacious, clean rooms offering all the standard amenities at an unbeatable price. *80 rooms | 678 Saded Rd | tel. 0 42 42 28 89 | www.royalnakhara.com | Budget*

WHERE TO GO

BAN CHIANG (129 D4) (𝑀 G5)

In 1966, a man in Ban Chiang accidentally tripped over some tree roots and fell down – no sensation there then. But the story doesn't end there. This U.S. American had in fact stumbled onto one of the oldest and most important prehistoric settlements in all of Southeast Asia. Half a century of excavations and research have revealed that in this village, 100 km/62 miles southeast of Nong Khai, lived, 3500 years ago, an advanced farming community which had mastered the art of bronze casting. Unesco added this archaeological find to its list of World Heritage Sites in 1992. Amongst the treasure trove of artefacts, archaeologists discovered metal items of jewellery such as bracelets and ankle rings, extremely pretty ceramics with fine wave and spiral patterns as well as human skeleton bones, all exhibited in the impressive ★ *National Museum (daily 8.30am–4.30pm | admission 150 baht)*. The excavation site itself is not a tourist destination but a small model of the site can be seen in the courtyard of *Wat Po Sri Nai*. Traders sell ceramic products in front of the museum. *www. penn.museum/banchiang*

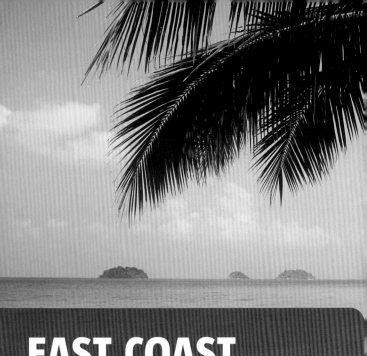

EAST COAST

Between Bangkok and the Cambodian border, 400 km (250 miles) of coastline await the visitors. Apart from the bustling international tourist playground of Pattaya, there are many smaller places at which to spend a relaxing beach holiday.

Heading east from Bangkok along Hwy 3, you'll pass through Thailand's largest industrial region, the Eastern Seaboard. But once you pass the salt ponds in Chonburi, the scenery starts to improve, and the holiday atmosphere returns completely. While tourists all over the world sun themselves on the beaches of Pattaya, at weekends and holidays those of Rayong are invaded almost exclusively by city-weary Thais. Beyond Rayong, for tourists a rather unappealing provincial capital, fishermen and fruit growers once more have the fertile coastal strip all to themselves. You will encounter only two more cities on the journey, Chanthaburi, famous for its gemstones, and Trat, a springboard to Ko Chang. The second largest Thai island after Phuket (154,8 sq km/60 sq miles) is one of the most beautiful places on the East Coast of the Gulf of Thailand for a beach holiday – with or without the hype, whichever you prefer.

KO CHANG

(135 E–F4) (*M F11*) Wild and enticing, peaks rising to 744 m (2,441 ft), a

Bustle or calm under the palms: the tourist capital Pattaya and the island of Ko Chang are vacation worlds apart

few fishing villages and palm-fringed beaches: this is the jungle island of ⭐ Ko Chang.

Even well into the 1990s Ko Chang was the secret haunt of backpack tourists. It is only in the last 20 years or so that especially Thais, Chinese and Russians have arrived and the resort resembles a tourist fairground. By now, a tarmac road has leads along the beaches and through the jungle, and an undersea cable provides electricity from the nearby mainland. Resorts have sprung up like mushrooms. But on Ko Chang, you can still truly unwind. Some head directly to the beautiful remote islands in the archipelago with the same name and go island-hopping. *Ko Wai, Ko Mak* and *Ko Kut* are islands where you can experience your own holiday Robinsonade. Most visitors now arrive on Ko Chang and the 50 other islands via the two large piers of *Ao Thammachat* and *Centre Point,* approx. 15 km/9.3 miles west of Laem Ngob. The best is to inform yourself of the various travel possibilities when you are there. Ferry connections can be found at *www.kohchangferries. com*.

SIGHTSEEING

Ko Chang is situated in a national marine park, where nature is still the biggest attraction. In the jungle, tired hikers can refresh themsleves at several waterfalls, the most beautiful of which is the three-tiered *Tan Mayom (admis-*

FOOD & DRINK

You will find the majority of independent restaurants on White Sand Beach. For breakfast with a view and everything from sausages in spicy sauce to green Thai curry, head to ☆ *Paul's Restaurant (Moderate–Expensive)*. At night, the beach becomes a barbecue area as the resorts roll out mats for their guests and put up tables in the sand. A good, yet inexpensive option

Ko Chang has preserved much of its older, non-commercial charm

sion 200 baht) on the east coast near the park headquarters. You will only see water cascading down the three tiers during or just after the rainy season. The same goes for the *Klong Plu* waterfall *(admission 200 baht)* up behind Klong Phrao Beach. The fishing village of *Bang Bao* on the southern coast of the island was built on stilts in the sea. It is just the place for savouring fresh fish in an open-air restaurant right by the water.

in the shade of the trees is *Sangtawan (Budget–Moderate)*.

BEACHES

KAI BAE BEACH
The almost 2.5 km/1.5 mile long partially pebbled beach is said to be the most natural on the island. Behind it there is a pedestrian street with shops and pubs and a great ☆ lookout point on the southern end of the bay.

KLONG PHRAO BEACH

At almost 6 km (4 miles) this is the longest beach on the island with gently sloping sand. It's also the location of the largest resorts, all of them very peaceful since they're off the main road. But tourist infrastructure is rapidly being developed along the road.

LONELY BEACH (HAT THA NAM)

This beach is very pebbly with only a few hundred metres of sand, but with its zany chill-out bars and the cheapest accomodation on the island it is the place to go for backpack tourists helping to revive the hippie era. You'll need to hurry though: the first luxury resorts have already opened.

WHITE SAND BEACH (HAT SAI KAO)

White Sand Beach in the north is the island's main beach: a narrow, 2.5 km/1.5 mile long strip of flatland between the jungle-covered mountains and the sea. Even at low tide it is not as flat as the beaches further south. The beach road is built up with resorts, bars, shops and travel agencies.

SPORTS & ACTIVITIES

Diving is increasingly popular, but even if you're only interested in snorkelling, you can still go along on a dive boat. Kayaks can be rented on the beach. Cruises to the surrounding islands and trekking tours through the jungle can be booked at any travel agency. In the village of ⚙ INSIDER TIP *Salak Kok* on the east coast, the locals have started an initiative to preserve the Mangrove jungle. A ⚫ *Mangrove nature trail (free admission)* with English information boards takes you through this fascinating ecosystem. At high tide, you can also paddle through the mangroves in a kayak *(100–200 baht per hour)*. Alternatively, sail across the crowns of the trees on ropes or hanging bridges at the *Tree Top Adventure Park (www.treetopadventurepark.com)* in the interior of the island.

ENTERTAINMENT

A few of the more unusual beach bars on White Sand Beach and Lonely Beach only close once the last guest has left. Long chains of fairy lights wound around bushes and palm trees as well as the usual fire artists create a festive atmosphere. Popular meeting places are the *Sabay Bar* (full moon parties, live music) and *Oodie's Place* (live music) opposite. The restaurant terrace at ⚫ INSIDER TIP *Rock Sand Resort*, set on a rocky outcrop at the northern end of White Sand Beach, is the best locale for enjoying a sundowner. One exclusive address is the trendy cocktail beach bar *Mojito Lounge* with dancefloor at Kai Bae Beach. Lonely Beach with its backpacker scene is known as the party beach of Ko Chang. If you

⭐ **Ko Chang**
A lot of beaches, a lot of jungle and resorts for all budgets
→ p. 65

⭐ **Pattaya**
Numerous excursion destinations and activities: the city on the Gulf of Thailand has much more to offer than bars
→ p. 69

⭐ **Chanthaburi**
Where precious gems are cut: day tours to the sapphire mines with a stopover at a mountain monastery → p. 73

MARCO POLO HIGHLIGHTS

Strip of sand between the jungle and the sea: White Sand Beach

enjoy a lively nightlife, you've come to the right place.

WHERE TO STAY

Ko Chang is booming. Accommodation is scarce during peak season from December to February, so book well in advance. The prices here are still modest by Thai standards.

BANPU KO CHANG RESORT
A virtual South Sea paradise: palm-thatched bungalows with TV, mini bar and a small pool – in the midst of a tropical garden on White Sand Beach. *31 rooms | mobile tel. 08 19 35 69 53 | www. banpuresort.com | Expensive*

CENTARA KO CHANG TROPICANA RESORT
A very scenic facility in a tropical garden on Klong Phrao Beach. Spacious and stylish bungalows with every modern convenience, two pools. *157 rooms | tel. 0 39 55 71 22 | www.centarahotelsresorts. com | Expensive*

KLONG PRAO RESORT
Well-maintained bungalows (with TV and refrigerator) along a lagoon, only a few metres from the beach, plenty of space on the landscaped grounds. Reasonably priced, many regulars – for 30 years now. *126 rooms | tel. 0 39 55 11 16 | www.klong praoresort.com | Budget–Moderate*

PAJAMAS KOH CHANG HOSTEL
This stylish hostel on Klong Phrao Beach offers comfortable rooms as well as cheap beds with curtains in the air-conditioned dormitory plus a pretty pool. *22 rooms | tel. 0 39 51 07 89 | www.pajamas kohchang.com | Moderate*

PORNS BUNGALOWS ☼
Who needs a TV here? Every evening, the sun presents a blood-red spectacle.

A rustic resort right on Kai Bae Beach, shaded by old broad-leaved trees and coconut palms. A hot spot for travellers. Most of the modest bungalows are made of wood and bamboo mats and have their own showers and ventilators; there are also a few stone chalets with air conditioning. It has a popular terrace restaurant *(Budget)* thanks to the authentic, cheap and delicious food so you'll have to share this small piece of paradise with others. *26 rooms | www.pornsbungalows-kohchang.com | Budget*

INFORMATION

TOURISM AUTHORITY OF THAILAND
To the left in front of Laem Ngob Pier | tel. 0 39 59 72 55

WHERE TO GO

OASIS SEA WORLD (135 E3) *(ಐ F10)*
This is where you can swim with dolphins – but only if you have short fingernails and leave your glasses and jewellery behind (dolphins have sensitive skin!). The breeding station is located approx. 50 km (31 miles) west of Trat in Laem Sing. Dolphins that have been injured or tangled in nets are nursed back to health at the facility. Since there is a limited number of visitors permitted, booking in advance is highly recommended. *Admission 300 baht (including the show), 2500 baht for swimming with the dolphins | several travel agencies also offer day tours | tel. 0 39 49 92 22 | www.swimwithdolphinsthailand.com*

PATTAYA

(134 C3) *(ಐ D10)* **Both famous and infamous, and written off by the media numerous times, ★ Pattaya is now** **more lively than ever. Nothing now remains of the sleepy fishing village that existed here in the 1960s – except for the name "The Village" for what is arguably Thailand's most famous red light district.**

With a population of 300,000, Pattaya is a pulsating city which never stops. With its 1000 restaurants and 2000 hotels and hostels, this city of superlatives boasts some excellent places to stay and eat for the millions of tourists who visit the city every year. The *Pattaya Park Tower (345 Jomtien Beach | tel. 0 38 25 12 01 | www.pattayapark.com/tower.html | Moderate–Expensive)* has a revolving panoramic restaurant at a height of 174 m/570 ft and invites anyone brave enough to freestyle abseil down from the 55th floor. With its gigantic shopping malls and water slides, Pattaya promises action and amusement all the way. The hundreds of bars and go-go clubs, which once gave Pattaya its reputation as sin city, are now tourist attractions and the authorities are cracking down on child prostitution. The once polluted Bay of Pattaya has also become cleaner thanks to a water treatment facility. A yacht

> **CITY** **WHERE TO START?**
> **Central Festival Shopping Centre:** The shopping centre in the middle of Beach Rd in the centre of Pattaya is an ideal starting point for exploring the bay to the north and to the south. Baht buses (pick-ups with benches) drive down Beach Rd then back up along the parallel Second Rd (put your hand out to hail the bus, press the bell button to disembark; bus fare 10 baht, 20 baht at night). These two main roads have the most shops, restaurants, and hotels.

harbour, sky-rises accommodating luxury hotel chains and beach promenades have given the city a modern facelift.

For sunbathing and swimming around Pattaya, most holidaymakers head out of the city to *Jomtien Beach* with its miles of sand (10 minutes away by taxi) and the *Golden Beach* or north of Pattaya to the small beach in the district of *Naklua* and to *Wongamat Beach*. Further south of Pattaya and outside the city at Bang Saray, there are two good beaches *Ban Amphur* and *Sunset Beach*. Besides extreme and fun sports, Pattaya also offers 'normal' activities such as golf, diving, sailing, fishing, bowling, tennis, rifle-shooting, horseriding, go-karting – pretty much everything.

On the floating market in Pattaya

The list of tourist attractions in the province of Chonburi, where Pattaya is situated, is seemingly endless: offshore islands, sea aquarium, botanical gardens, folklore shows – one holiday is not nearly enough to see everything.

MINI SIAM

Fancy a little world trip? In Mini Siam, it takes only two to three hours: The large park showcases the most famous buildings in Thailand and the rest of the world on a 1:25 scale, brightly illuminated in the evening. *Daily 7am–10pm | admission 300 baht, including pick-up service at tel. 0 38 72 73 33 on Sukhumvit Hwy., near the Bangkok Hospital Pattaya | www. minisiam.com*

PATTAYA FLOATING MARKET

The lake is artificial, likewise the stilt village in the middle of it. Although it was entirely designed for tourists, the Floating Market almost seems like a relic from the past – yet with modern adrenaline boosters like ziplines and crocodile canapés on a stick. There are also more than 100 restaurants and shops, which are interconnected by bridges. *Daily 9am–8pm | admission from 200 baht, boat tours 800 baht | in southeast Pattaya, in the direction of Jomtien on the Sukhumvit Hwy. | www.pattayafloating market.com*

RIPLEY'S BELIEVE IT OR NOT ●

Anything that is unbelievable, yet true, is on display here: from a three-legged horse to a mask made out of human skin to a Titanic constisting of 1 million matches. *Daily 11am–11pm | admission 500 baht (online ticket) | in the Royal Garden Plaza Shopping Centre (at the centre of Pattaya) | www.ripleysthailand.com*

SANCTUARY OF TRUTH

Gods, ghosts, goosepimples – here you'll mingle with lots of mythical creatures. The world's tallest teak building lies in Naklua Bay and impresses with thousands of carved figures based on Far Eastern mythologies and religions. The 100-m long and 100-m high monument is a private art and life's work. No nails and no metal were used when the structure was built. *Daily 8am–6pm | admission 450 baht (online ticket) | 206 Naklua Rd, Soi 12 | www.sanctuaryoftruth.com*

FOOD & DRINK

BRUNO'S

An elegant restaurant with Swiss management serving excellent Mediterranean and Thai cuisine. *306/63 Chateau Dale Plaza | Thappraya Rd | Jomtien Beach | tel. 038 36 46 00 | www.brunos-pattaya.com | Expensive*

INSIDER TIP MANTRA

With everything from sushi and tandoori to bouillabaisse, the culinary delights of the East and the West come together here and are cooked before your eyes in the open kitchen. Tastefully decorated, plus a very appealing ambiance and excellent service to top it all off! Which means everything has its (western) price... *Beach Rd | near Soi 1 at the Amari Hotel | tel. 038 42 95 91 | www.mantra-pattaya.com | Expensive*

RUEN THAI RESTAURANT

Guests are entertained with classical Thai dancing. This open-air restaurant is a classic among tourists and dishes have been adapted to cater for visitors' tastes over the years. So if you're new to Thailand, don't worry: even the green Thai curry isn't too hot at Ruen Thai. *Pattaya 2 Rd | South Pattaya | tel.*

Wood carvings at the Sanctuary of Truth

038 42 59 11 | www.ruenthairestaurant.com | Moderate

SHOPPING

Central Festival between Beach Rd and Second Rd offers the ultimate shopping experience: a gigantic emporium with 200 shops, restaurants, food stalls and cafés, an enormous supermarket, 16 bowling lanes and the luxury multiplex ● *SFX Cinema* with 10 screens. You will also find an array of shops and boutiques at the nearby *Royal Garden Plaza*. The *Mike Shopping Mall (262 Pattaya 2nd Rd)* is a large department store that resembles a covered bazaar.

ENTERTAINMENT

Pattaya has a host of pubs with live music. The most popular clubs can be found on

Walking Street: *Club Insomnia*, the modern *Mixx Discotheque (Bali Hai Plaza)* and the almost legendary, gloomy *Marine Disco*. For sophisticated cocktails with a view of the city, take the lift to the 34th floor of the Hilton Pattaya, home of the ❧ *Horizon Rooftop Bar (333/101 Beach Rd)*. For a completely different kind of experience with impressive costumes and spectacular stage sets, hit one of the travesty revues at ● *Tiffany's Show (admission 800–1200 baht | 464 Pattaya 2nd Rd | tel. 038 42 17 00 | www.tiffany-show.co.th)* and at the *Alcazar (admission 600–800 baht | 78/14 Pattaya 2nd Rd | tel. 0 38 42 22 20 | www.alcazarthailand. com)*.

WHERE TO STAY

HOTEL BARAQUDA PATTAYA – M GALLERY BY SOFITEL

The design hotel is one of the hippest and most popular hotels in Pattaya. The spacious rooms have a contemporary and cool interior – 80s feeling! The ❧ restaurant on the seventh floor enjoys a fantastic view. *72 rooms | Pattaya 2nd Rd | tel. 0 38 76 99 99 | www.hotelba raquda.com | Expensive*

THAI GARDEN RESORT

Renowned child-friendly facility (playground, children's menus) with a large pool area and comfortable rooms as well as bread and cake from their own bakery. Five minutes by taxi to Wong Amat Beach. *217 rooms | 179 North Pattaya Rd | tel. 0 38 37 06 14 | www. thaigarden.com | Moderate–Expensive*

LE VIMAN RESORT

Small and cosy place for self-catering guests: The house is like a tranquil oasis in the middle of a residential area. Jungle-inspired garden with pool and elegant apartments. Under French management. *12 rooms | Moo 10 | Tappraya Rd, Soi 15 | mobile tel. 08 00 90 29 32 | www. vimanresort.com | Moderate*

Pattaya buzzes with life at night under the neon lights of Walking Street

TOURISM AUTHORITY OF THAILAND
Pratamnak Rd | direction Jomtien Beach | tel. 0 38 42 87 50

WHERE TO GO

CHANTHABURI ★
(135 E3) (*ⁿ F10*)

The provincial capital (pop. 40,000) 170 km (106 miles) southeast of Pattaya is famed for its sapphires and rubies. Most of the mines have been worked out and are now closed, but you can still see gem cutters and traders at work on the gemstone market. Although many stones today come from Cambodia, Chanthaburi remains a centre of the Thai gemstone trade. The French-style *Notre Dame* cathedral, the largest in the country, is also worth seeing. At the end of the 19th century, Vietnamese Christians emigrated to Chanthaburi and introduced the colonial style which is still evident today in many houses. A stopover at the *Wat Kao Sukim* mountain monastery and the waterfall at *Khitchakut National Park* make an ideal day tour. *Tour from Pattaya incl. lunch approx. 1800 baht*

KO LARN (134 C3) (*ⁿ D10*)

Just 8 km (5 miles) from Pattaya, this island of 4 sq km (1.5 sq miles), with its white sandy beaches and clean water, is a popular local island excursion; there's quite a lot going on there. Travel agencies book island tours with excursion boats. Chartered speedboats will whisk you across for approx. 1500–2500 baht. The regular ferry from INSIDER TIP▶ *Bali Hai Pier* in South Pattaya costs only 30 baht.

KO SAMET (135 D3) (*ⁿ E10*)

The 20 sq km (8 sq mile) island is located 80 km (50 miles) southeast of Pattaya in the Gulf of Thailand and is part of a Marine Sanctuary *(admission 200 baht)*. Its scenic sandy beaches lure hordes of visitors from Bangkok on weekends. There are plenty of bungalow complexes, including the recommendable and appealing *Vongduean Resort (64 rooms | tel. 0 38 64 41 71 | www.vrresortkohsamed. com | Moderate–Expensive)*, situated on the beautiful beach of the same name, that offers a free ferry service. *Minibuses take you to the fishing village Ban Phe for approx. 250–350 baht | ferry trips 50–100 baht (crossing takes 30 minutes)*

LOW BUDGET

Air-conditioned buses depart for Pattaya every 30 minutes from the Ekkamai bus station in Bangkok (right by Ekkamai Skytrain station). A single journey costs 140 baht. A slower but less costly option (30 baht) is the train from the Bangkok main train station at 6.50am. A joint ticket for buses and ferries *(www.12go.asia)* will take you from Bangkok to the Ko Chang archipelago islands for around 450 baht.

Your French hosts at the *Elephant Bay Resort (26 rooms | Bailan Bay | mobile tel. 09 88 36 36 93 | www.ele phantbayresort.com)* on Ko Chang always have a friendly ear and advice for their guests. Hammocks on the rocky beach, hostel-style bungalows, rows of rooms, some with air-conditioning and TV, and the best feature: a pool surrounded by palm trees – all this for just 600–1400 baht a night.

THE SOUTH

On the beaches and especially on the islands in the Gulf of Thailand and the Andaman Sea, holiday dreams come true for visitors from all over the world. Nature has smiled upon the Thai people from the South. Even before the tourists arrived they enjoyed a life of relative ease: plenty of fish from the seas, fertile land as well as considerable mineral wealth (notably tin) endowed the region with prosperity and even affluence.

KHAO LAK

(136 C4) (*A15*) Dreaming of beach and island hopping? Khao Lak is famous for its endlessly long, palm-fringed golden beaches hugging its 12 km/7.5 mile stretch of coastline. Sandy bliss can be enjoyed at Khao Lak, also known as Sunset Beach, Nang Thong, Bang Niang and Khuk Kak. The area also includes the offshore, still relatively pristine islands.

This stretch of paradise seems to have recovered from the tragedy which hit Khao Lak especially hard at Christmas of 2004 when the tsunami engulfed the area. Today, the resort is flourishing more than ever before, courtesy in part to Phuket airport which lies just 80 km/50 miles away. Memorials to this disaster include a *marine police boat (main road at Bang Niang Beach)* which was swept on land by the tsunami and a huge international *Tsunami Memorial (free admission | Ban Nam Khem | ap-*

A vacation paradise above and below water: fantastic beaches, fascinating dive sites and jungle tours

prox. 25 km/16 miles north of Khao Lak). The holiday region was restored for business at record speed. Warning sirens, rescue towers and evacuation signs are in place today to ensure visitor safety. The national route 4 runs parallel to the strip of coast with its splendid, yet today consistently expensive hotels. The road is lined with diving shops, restaurants and stores selling every holiday item imaginable from neon-green cocktails to bright pink smartphone cases.

FOOD & DRINK

BISTRO

Swiss people will be left longing for home, all others will enjoy the great food. The Swiss proprietor Nick serves homemade bread for breakfast and tempting cakes. *Main road to Bang Niang Beach | mobile tel. 08 62 77 09 19 | Budget–Moderate*

KHAOLAK SEAFOOD FAMILY HOUSE

The main income of this family run place is renting bungalows but it also

Dive down into the underwater world of the Similan Islands

does a great sideline in cooking up tasty fish dishes. *Nang Thong Beach | tel. 0 76 48 53 18 | www.khaolakseafood.com | Moderate*

SPORTS & ACTIVITIES

One of the world's best diving spots is only 50 km (31 miles) away: the *Similan Islands,* reached from *Tap Lamu pier* south of Khao Lak. The excellent diving areas further north around the *Surin Islands* (60 km/37 miles from the mainland) are also quick to reach from Khao Lak.

You can book tours to islands, caves and waterfalls in the jungle, such as the five-tiered and 200 m high (656 ft) INSIDER TIP ▶ *Chong Fah* in *Lamru National Park (daily 8am–4.30pm | admission 200 baht),* at travel agencies. Bang Niang Beach is also home to a *mini golf course (turn off the main road after the Tsunami Museum).*

ENTERTAINMENT

Night life in Khao Lak is mostly limited to looking up at the starry sky. Millenniums looking to party with local Thais should head to the *Build Factory (Bang Niang Beach | daily 6pm–2am),* the only night club in Khao Lak where the party only really gets going after midnight. The cosy *Monkey Bar (Bang Niang Beach)* and *Happy Snapper (daily from 22pm | Nang Thong Beach)* both offer live music. The *Moo Moo Cabaret (Mon, Wed, Thu, Sat 7.15pm, 9.45pm, Tue, Fri, Sun 9.45pm)* is not quite as grand as the travesty shows in Phuket or Pattaya, but there is no cover charge.

WHERE TO STAY

Khao Lak is not ideal for budget travellers: you won't find a room on the beach for less than approx. 750 baht.

LA FLORA RESORT & SPA

A world-class resort with a range of luxurious rooms as perfectly styled as the whole complex. Beautiful pool and spa. *138 rooms | Bang Niang Beach | tel. 0 76 42 80 00 | www.lafloraresort.com | Expensive*

GREEN BEACH RESORT

Simple, clean bungalows – all air-conditioned, with mini-bar and bamboo furniture – set in a scenic garden. The bungalows are placed rather close together, though this is the most reasonably priced resort for its beach location. *44 rooms | Nang Thong Beach | tel. 0 76 48 58 45 | www.khaolakgreen beachresort.com | Moderate*

INSIDER TIP▶ POSEIDON BUNGALOWS ☻

Ideal for those seeking peace and quiet in modest bungalows (shower, fan) between the jungle and the beach. A small, eco-friendly hideaway, no trees were felled for the bungalows' construction, they grow through your verandah. Bio-degradable waste is composted, and non-returnable bottles are frowned upon. The rustic huts could do with a new coat of paint, though. The owners organise diving tours to the Similan Islands. *15 rooms | turnoff at km 53 (32 miles) from the direction of Phuket | mobile tel. 08 78 95 92 04 | www.simila ntour.com | Budget*

WHERE TO GO

TAKUA PA OLD TOWN
(136 C4) (*Ø B14*)

The small town of Takua Pa is a half-hour drive north of Khao Lak. It is divided into the bustling new town with a large market, and the sleepy *Old Town* providing a reminder of Takua Pa's glorious past, when, during the height of the tin boom in the 19th century it even had a stint as the provincial capital. The many old buildings, built in Chinese and Sino-Portuguese style, testify to the town's former wealth, even if they have seen better days.

MARCO POLO HIGHLIGHTS

★ **Khao Sok National Park**
Unbridled nature and adventure in a primeval jungle setting → p. 78

★ **Ko Lanta**
Plenty of beach for everyone – the further south, the quieter → p. 78

★ **Ko Jum**
The tiny jungle island allows your spirit to flow → p. 80

★ **Ko Samui**
Feasting and sports, clubbing and chilling on the island of coconut palms → p. 80

★ **Phuket**
Where VIPs and travellers from all over the world meet: Thailand's diving centre and first class beaches as well as great views from the Big Buddha and the lighthouse on Cape Promthep → p. 87

★ **Phang Nga Bay**
Stunning: rocky islands, stalactite caves and a stilt village in the sea → p. 91

★ **Ko Phi Phi**
Spectacular and cinematic: Phi Phi Don and Phi Phi Le are Thailand's most beautiful islands → p. 90

KHAO SOK NATIONAL PARK ★
(140 C4) (*Ⓜ B14*)

Real-life jungle camp offering spectacular and intrepid adventures and a kind of survival training: Can you survive 48 hours without WiFi? Located 90 km/56 miles northeast of Khao Lak, this national park is the oldest evergreen rainforest with its 60 million year-old limestone mountains, stalactite caves and waterfalls. Listen at close range to the summing of the cicadas (reaching up to 120 decibels), which sound like a whistling kettle and if you're lucky you may hear the love calls of the gibbons at dawn. You can also get a taste of adventure by trying various activities such as tubing, kayak tours or rafting. Day tours are offered everywhere in Khao Lak. One of the MARCO POLO discovery tours (see p. 99) also takes you into the "jungle of the gigantic flower". *Visitor centre daily 8am–4.30pm | admission 300 baht | national road 401, junction at km 109*

KO LANTA

(138 A3) (*Ⓜ B16*) **Fishing villages, rainforest, splendid beaches and tiny islands perfect for island hopping or diving: situated in the deep south, ★ Ko Lanta is a tranquil place and mostly Muslim. You may even hear the cries of the Muezzin early morning.**

In the village of Ban Saladan, where the ferries dock, you'll find souvenir shops, tailors, cafés, travel agencies and dive shops. Ferries from Phuket, Ko Phi Phi and Krabi will get you to Ko Lanta Yai in one and a half to four hours; if you're prone to get seasick, you can also take the minibuses from Krabi via the neighbouring island of Ko Lanta Noi (about two and a half hours). This shortens the route travelled on ferries.

FOOD & DRINK

Ban Saladan has several seafood restaurants occupying houses built on stilts over the water. Bakery/café *Nang Sabai German Bakery (daily 7.30–5pm)* on the main road 1 km south of the town offers German bread and delicious cakes. The beach bar 🌐 *Same Same But Different (mobile tel. 08 17 87 86 70 | Budget–Moderate)*, at Kantiang Bay, serves international and vegan cuisine.

BEACHES

All bathing beaches are situated on the 20-km (13-mile) long west coast of Ko Lanta Yai. As a rule of thumb, the further south you travel the quieter it gets. The last two beaches in the bays of *Klong Jak* and INSIDER TIP *Mai Pai (Bamboo Bay),* which are reached along a partly steep road, are virtually untouched by tourism.

SPORTS & ACTIVITIES

The resorts and travel agencies provide jungle and mangrove tours as well as snorkelling excursions and caving. Ban Saladan has numerous dive shops (an overview of the best diving spots can be found at: *www.lantainfo.com*).

The villagers of 🌐 *Tung Yee Peng (tours from the travel agency approx. 1000 baht)* want to integrate tourism into their daily lives without destroying their natural environment. Boat tours into the mangroves operated by the locals will give you the chance to get to know the ecosystem from which the islanders have lived for many generations. In Tung Yee Peng you can enjoy simple accommodation and immerse yourself in village life.

Trendy meeting places at Long Beach include the *Ozone Bar* (beach partys on Thursdays) and *Funky Monkey* – that is, if you like karaoke partys and drinking mojitos from buckets. Or catch the fire shows at several beach bars in the evenings. Information on current events at *www.fb.com/groups/lanta.*

WHERE TO STAY

BAMBOO BAY RESORT

Modest hillside bungalows. A fine cliff-top restaurant with ☀ views over the

either be repulsed or delighted by their architecture. Expansive premises and a large pool. *22 rooms | Klong Dao Beach | tel. 0 75 66 81 86 | www.costalanta.com |* *Expensive*

INSIDER TIP ▸ LAYANA

This is how to start into a perfect holiday morning: breakfast on the wide beach! This elegant resort provides guestrooms in luxurious pavillions, a spa, a stunning ☀ saltwater pool with a view of the sea, a huge open-air jacuzzi and fitness area. Also friendly and professional staff. *51 rooms | Long Beach | tel. 0 75 60 71 00 | www.layanaresort.com | Expensive*

Time for a snack? The market of Ban Saldan on Ko Lanta has plenty of spicy options

secluded bay. *21 rooms | Bamboo Bay | tel. 0 75 66 50 23 | Budget*

COSTA LANTA

Minimalist upscale bungalows constructed of concrete and old wood are surrounded by high casuarina trees. You'll

NICE'N EASY HOUSE

This nice mini resort is situated in a slightly hidden place, but directly on the beach. You can stay in air-conditioned wooden bungalows or in rooms at the terraced house. A small pool provides refreshment during the daytime. *10 rooms |*

Klong Khong Beach | tel. 08 14 76 65 46 | www.niceandeasylanta.com | Moderate

WHERE TO GO

KO JUM ⭐ ● (138 A2) (*∅ B16*)
This 9-km (5.6-miles) long island (20 km/13 miles north of Ko Lanta) is in the shadow of the main tourism developments, but has still benefited from the Lanta boom. There are a couple of dozen small resorts here. Known in its northern part as Ko Pu, it is an island of jungle and rubber plantations; there is one paved road leading from north to south, the power poles were only erected in 2010. Today, the main village of *Ban Ko Jum* in the far south will supply you with all your daily needs. For your journey to Ko Jum, take the ferry from Krabi to Lanta, where longtail boats pick up travellers. *New Bungalow (27 rooms | Andaman Beach | mobile tel. 08 97 26 26 52 | www.kohjumonline.com/new.html | Budget)* offers modest bungalows with or without showers. Englishman Ray and his wife, Sao, operate the pleasant *Woodland Lodge (14 rooms, equipped with showers | Andaman Beach | mobile tel. 08 18 93 53 30 | www.woodland-koh-jum.com | Budget)* noted for its outstanding cuisine. Located on a scenic hillside you'll find the INSIDER TIP *Oonlee Bungalows (9 rooms | Kidong Beach | mobile tel. 08 72 00 80 53 | www.kohjumoonleebungalows.com | Budget–Expensive)*. Valerie (Lee), originally from France, and her husband, Oon, ensure a pleasant ambience to accompany their appetising meals. The *Freedom Bar* and the *Coco Bar* at the southern end of Andaman Beach are both beach bars with a campfire.

KO SAMUI

(137 E3) (*∅ C14*) ⭐ **Ko Samui is Thailand's third-largest island (population: 50,000). As you approach by air, the impression is of one massive coconut plantation crowned by a jungle-covered mountain. Even the little airport has a rustic feel, at first glance looking more like a beach resort.**

However, this once hippie island cannot halt the change: cool designer hostels with poolside villas, luxury spas and nightclubs are popping up all over to

---

LOW BUDGET

Bamboo huts on the beaches have become a rarity in the South. Great location directly on the beach:

Ko Samui: *Spa Samui Beach (mobile tel. 09 94 06 4503 | www.thesparesorts.net)* at Lamai Beach still has some old A Frame bungalows with showers and fans, some with air conditioning from 825 baht.

Phuket: *Ao Sane Bungalows (tel. 0 76 28 83 06)*, equipped with cold showers, is located in one of the most beautiful coves (Ao Sane). The food is better elsewhere. From 470 baht.

Ko Lanta: *Where Else (mobile tel. 09 3293 65 45 | www.whereellselanta.com)* at Long Beach could easily pass for a set from a hippie movie. Huts with showers, WC with bucket flush and fans from 450 baht.

Ko Jum: *Bo Daeng Bungalows (mobile tel. 08 14 94 87 60)* at Andaman Beach has huts with and without showers from 150 baht.

On a higher level: Big Buddha, the landmark of Ko Samui

accommodate tourists from around the world.

SIGHTSEEING

The 247 sq km (95 sq mile) island can be explored in a day via its 51-km (32-mile) long ring road – which weaves around the steep coastline past beaches and secluded tiny bays. On the way you will pass two of the island's famous rocks: *Hin Ta* and *Hin Yai* at the southern end of Lamai beach. The "Grandmother rock" and the "Grandfather rock" have the shape of male and female genitalia and are a popular photo spot, not only for the rather prudish Thais. Local legend has it that an elderly couple were drowned when shipwrecked off the coast, turning into rocks.

In the south of the island it is well worth taking a detour up into the mountains to the **INSIDER TIP** *Secret Buddha Garden (Tarnim Magic Garden) (daily 10am–5pm | admission 80 baht)* near the Tarnim waterfall, a magical world of weathered Buddha statues set in a rocky jungle landscape. Equally worthwhile is a trip to the island's landmark, the 12-m (39-ft) high *Big Buddha,* as well as the *Hin Lat* and *Namuang waterfalls.*

FOOD & DRINK

Thai cuisine from food stalls such as those at the *Lamai Food Center (night market from 5pm)* or in neighbourhood restaurants is often better (and less expensively) prepared than in restaurants that cater to tourists. At Chaweng

the Anantara Resort. Excellent, authentic Italian meals are served at INSIDER TIP ▶ *Duomo (Soi Montien House | Chaweng Beach | tel. 0 77 30 05 04 | duomo-kohsa mui.business.site | Expensive).*

BEACHES

The most resorts and the best infrastructure with many restaurants can be found on ● *Chaweng Beach,* the most beautiful, and on *Lamai Beach* on the east coast. The bays of *Thong Sai, Choeng Mon, Chaweng Noi, Coral Cove* and *Na Khai* are small oases of tranquility. *Mae Nam, Bo Phut* and *Big Buddha* beaches on the north coast are likewise free of overwhelming tourist hype. The southern and western regions of Ko Samui are not especially attractive, and the shallow water is not really suitable for swimming.

SPORTS & ACTIVITIES

You have the choice of various aquatic sports on Ko Samui, the largest selection of which is found at Chaweng Beach and Lamai Beach, among them diving. There are mini-golf courses at Chaweng Beach and on the road from Choeng Mon to the Big Buddha Beach. If you're in the mood for a proper game of golf, the island has four full-length courses to choose from *(www.samui.sawadee.com/golf).*

ENTERTAINMENT

Chaweng Beach is the centre of the island's nightlife. At the disco classic *Green Mango(www.thegreenmangoclub. com),* there's a good vibe, but the drinks are watered down and you have to pay attention to your change. Beer and go-go bars are a few doors down. The atmosphere is more relaxed and rustic accompanied by reggae at *The Rock Bar*

Paradise in Thailand's South: Lamai Beach on Ko Samui

Beach, several resorts set up tables and chairs on the beach in the evening and grill seafood on charcoal fires. Foodies and romantics will feel like they are in paradise at the beautifully-situated restaurant *Tree Tops (Chaweng Beach | tel. 0 77 96 03 33 | lawana-chaweng.anantara. com/tree-tops | Expensive)* belonging to

(www.samuirockbar.com) on the beach. Travesty shows are put on at *Starz Cabaret (www.starzcabaret.com)*. For anyone looking for a quieter and more exclusive location: *Fisherman's Village* at Bo Phut Beach invites you to stroll around, take a bite to eat and sip cocktails. The beach is also the venue for the night market which opens every Friday at 5pm in Walking Street.

WHERE TO STAY

EDEN BUNGALOWS

Intimate resort with French management, set in a lush tropical garden with pool. The fully equipped rooms are either in bungalows or in the main Thai House. Two minutes away from the beach. *15 rooms | Bo Phut Beach | tel. 0 77 42 76 45 | www.edenbungalows.com | Moderate*

HARRY'S BUNGALOWS

Located at the northern end of Mae Nam Beach near the pier where the ferry departs for Ko Phangan, you will find plenty of greenery and tranquility around these very clean and cosy bungalows with air conditioning. *22 rooms | tel. 0 77 42 37 91 | www.harrys-samui.com | Budget*

LAMAI PERFECT RESORT

The resort is an excellent value for money. Guests stay in well-kept, spacious rooms with all the amenities. Splash around in the pool or walk two minutes to the beach. *30 rooms | Lamai Beach | tel. 0 77 42 44 06 | www.lamaiperfectresort.com | Budget*

THE LIBRARY

A cool design hotel: luxury rooms in white cubes, a red tiled pool, and plenty of green. Enjoy breakfast right on the beach on comfortable white mats. *26 rooms | Chaweng Beach | tel. 0 77 42 27 67 | www.thelibrarysamui.com | Expensive*

INFORMATION

TOURISM AUTHORITY OF THAILAND

Nathon | Chonvithee Rd | behind the post office | tel. 0 77 42 05 04

FOR BOOKWORMS & FILM BUFFS

The King and I – King Mongkut was unfairly portrayed as bad tempered and naïve in this fictionalised account of his court. The film is still banned in Thailand, along with the 1946 film "Anna and the King of Siam" and the more recent film "Anna and the King" starring Jodie Foster.

Nana Plaza – Christopher Moore took the title of his mystery novel from a bar district in Bangkok. Full of suspense and local colour.

The Beach – Director Danny Boyle filmed this drama with Leonardo Di Caprio on the island of Phi Phi Le. An exciting storyline with stunning landscape cinematography.

Ong-Bak – He is Thailand's absolute superstar: Tony Jaa, actor and kickboxer. In these cult flicks directed by Prachya Pin-kaew, he fights his way through Bangkok on the search for a stolen Buddha head.

ANG THONG NATIONAL PARK
(137 E3) (*C13–14*)

The archipelago of 40 uninhabited islands between Ko Samui and the mainland is ideal for snorkelling. Travel agencies offer day tours; one of the most interesting ones to consider is an exploration of the marine park by kayak. *300 baht*

KO PHANGAN (137 E3) (*C13–14*)

There's always a party going on somewhere. In terms of attractions, you'll be spoilt for choice with fire shows, yoga schools and kick-box camps. Ko Samui's neighbour (191 sq km/74 sq miles), reachable by ferry in 30 minutes, is a mountainous jungle in the sea surrounded by 30 (!) fine sandy beaches and picturesque small coves. A wild jungle beauty, Ko Phangan was once considered the destination for backpackers but has now been usurped by the mainstream tourist industry. More and more air-conditioned bungalows are replacing old palm leaf huts, while upscale resorts await more affluent travellers. A prime location

is the *Santhiya (99 rooms | Thong Nai Pan Noi Beach | tel. 0 77 42 89 99 | www. santhiya.com | Expensive).* Reasonably priced accommodation is still available at all beaches, for instance, the lovely, eco-conscious *Phangan Rainbow Bungalows (25 rooms | tel. 0 77 23 82 36 | www.rainbowbungalows.com | Budget)* on Ban Kai Beach where water is heated with solar energy. Ko Phangan's monthly *Full Moon Party (www.fullmoon. phangan.info)* is now world famous, attracting tens of thousands of revellers to *Rin Beach (Hat Rin).*

KO TAO (137 E2) (*C13*)

The waters around this former penal colony with its distinctive rounded granite peaks are said to provide the best diving in the entire Gulf of Thailand. The 21 sq km (8 sq mile) island boasts more than 40 dive shops from where enthusiasts fan out to 25 dive spots, to whale sharks and sea turtles.

There are a few upscale resorts here – such as the *Woodlawn Villas (8 rooms | Chalok Baan Khao | near Sai Ri Beach in a park | mobile tel. 08 44 45 96 72 | www. woodlawnvillas.com | Budget–Moder-*

Delve into the midst of 40 isolated islands on a kayak tour in Ang Thong National Park

ate). They even offer apartments with pool – at unbeatable prices. Plenty of more modest accommodation can be found on the main beaches of *Mae Hat* and *Sai Ri* as well as in small bays, e.g. the laid-back *Sairee Cottage (45 rooms | Sai Ri Beach | tel. 077456126 | www.saireecottagediving.com | Budget–Moderate)* with diving school on the premises. Ferries cross from the mainland (Chumphon) and from Ko Samui (via Ko Phangan).

KRABI

(138 A1–2) (*ⅅ B15–16*) **One attraction after the other awaits you in Krabi. This strip of coastline boasts spectacular mountains and some of the country's most beguiling beaches. However, word about its beauty has spread and you certainly won't be alone in this jungle-like landscape to the east of Phuket – during the main season probably not even on your own selfie.**

Spectacular limestone cliffs flank the prime beaches of *Phra Nang* and *Railay,* which are popular among travellers the world over and are only accessible by boat from the main beach *Ao Nang* in approx. 20 minutes. It is quieter on the beaches of *Klong Muang, Noppharat Thara* and *Tup Kaek,* as well as in *Ton Sai Bay.*

SIGHTSEEING

KRABI TOWN

The cosy provincial capital (pop. 26500) is situated at the estuary of the Krabi River. There is a selection of modest guesthouses as well as a few hotels, but so far the place hasn't been overrun by tourists. On the riverbank right in the centre you can charter a boat to explore the mangrove forests on the opposite bank. Fancy a detour to a remote magic forest? From Uttarakit Rd turn off along the INSIDER TIP *Mangrove Forest Walkway (Thapom Klongsongnam | admission 50 baht).* The boardwalk leads you approx. 400 m through a mangrove forest with impressively high roots. Even though the Thais do it, it's not advisable to bathe in the river here, however tempting the turquoise-coloured, milky water may be.

PHRA NANG CAVE AND PRINCESS LAGOON

In the ⬤ *Phra Nang Cave (free admission)* on Phra Nang Beach stands a shrine surrounded by huge wooden phalluses (lingams), a fertility symbol. People leave offerings here in order to be blessed with children or other good fortune. After an arduous ascent to the top of the 150-m (500-ft) high ⚡ cliffs, you can see the *Princess Lagoon* below, which at high tide is filled with seawater.

WAT TAM SUA ⚡

High up in Buddha's footsteps: Located 6 km (4 miles) north of Krabi Town, *Wat*

Tam Sua (Tiger Cave Temple) is a meditation monastery, partly integrated into the caves of the temple mountain. The biggest attraction is the climb up 1273 very steep steps to the top, where you can see Buddha's footprint – and INSIDER TIP breathtaking views worth every drop of sweat. *Daily 7.30am–4.30pm, only in appropriate clothing*

FOOD & DRINK

For good yet cheap food head to the night market in Krabi Town. Seafood restaurants line the beachside lane *Soi Sunset* at the narrow north end of Ao Nang Beach. The *Last Café* on the southern end of the beach has an idyllic location.

SPORTS & ACTIVITIES

Watersports enthusiasts have plenty of opportunities for diving and kayaking (list of diving centres at: *www.aonang.com*). Climbers can test their stamina on the towering limestone formations.

Courses for beginners are offered at Phra Nang Beach, Railay East and at Ton Sai Bay *(www.railay.com)*.

ENTERTAINMENT

Krabi beaches are not known for their nightlife. Travellers tend to meet at pubs in Railay East and in the *Freedom Bar* in Ton Sai's hinterland. That's also where full moon parties take place.

WHERE TO STAY

INSIDER TIP AO NANG HOME STAY

Like a second home: Mr Chang runs a very hospitable and family-style accommodation on Ao Nang Beach. The rooms are quite small, but immaculately clean, comfortable and well-kept. Located about ten minutes from the beach on foot. *6 rooms | Ao Nang Rd, Soi 11 | mobile tel. 08 17 32 12 73 | www. aonanghomestay.com | Budget–Moderate*

Krabi's coast shines with white sand, lush green jungles and the turquoise blue water of the ocean

DEE ANDAMAN HOTEL
Modern hotel in Krabi Town with spacious rooms including four-poster beds and balconies; pool. The Dee Andaman is one of the best hotels in the city and offers a good value for money. *30 rooms | 45/19 Rattanadilok Rd | tel. 075 62 07 79 | www.deeandamanhotel.com | Budget*

NAKAMANDA
Pure luxury in a beautiful oasis: resort with upscale bungalows surrounded by lush greenery and old trees. For the ultimate in luxury take one of the gigantic villas with own private pool. Spa and swimming pool for all guests. *39 rooms | Klong Muang Beach | tel. 075 62 82 00 | www.nakamanda.com | Expensive*

RAILEI BEACH CLUB
A real refuge from the crowds of day trippers on the Railay beaches. The beautifully furnished, teak-style private houses situated within a large park on the white sand beach are rented out to holidaymakers. *33 rooms | Railay West Beach | mobile tel. 08 66 85 93 59 | www.raileibeachclub.com | Expensive*

INFORMATION

TOURISM AUTHORITY OF THAILAND
Krabi Town | 292 Maharat Rd | tel. 075 62 21 63

PHUKET

(136 C5–6) (*꒰B15–16*) It's no surprise that ★ Phuket (pop. 500,000) has become Asia's number one holiday island. Where else are there so many superlatives in one single place?
With 543 sq km/210 sq miles, it is Thailand's largest island, a true visitors' magnet with millions of tourists. Dozens of first-class, pearly white beaches. The largest agglomeration of restaurants, bars, dive centres, first-class accomodation and boutique hotels. And last but not least, what is left of its rainforest.

SIGHTSEEING

BIG BUDDHA ⬤ 〰
The 45-m (148-ft) high Buddha sitting atop the *Nakkerd* hill is Thailand's tallest Buddha and the island's new landmark. There is still some building work going on, but that doesn't diminish the view over Phuket's east coast. *Free admission | shortly after Chalong on the road to the airport (signposted)*

KAO PHRA THAEO NATURE RESERVE
Located in the north of Phuket, this park contains the only remaining virgin rainforest on the island. A hiking trail leads to waterfalls. At the ⬤ *Gibbon Rehabilitation Center (Sun–Fri 9am–4.30pm, Sun 9am–3pm | free amission, donation welcome | www.gibbonproject.org)*, gibbons abused as pets are prepared for a return to their natural habitat. *Daily 8am–5pm | admission 200 baht*

CAPE PROMTHEP 〰
Tourists by the busload clamour to photograph the sunset from the southernmost point of the island. Avoid the melee and go up to *Promthep Cape Restaurant (tel. 076 28 80 84 | Moderate)* and enjoy the view. The ⬤ *lighthouse (free admission)* at the cape offers the best panorama.

PHUKET AQUARIUM
You are surrounded by sharks, giant sea perch and countless small fish (in a glass tunnel)! Experience the sublime flora and fauna from the waters of Phuket up close. *Admission 180 baht | southeast of*

Phuket Town/Kap Phan Wa | www.phuket aquarium.org

PHUKET TOWN

Many old villas and commercial buildings in Sino-Portuguese style as well as Chinese-style temples still stand in the attractive town centre (pop. 60,000); they recall the era of the rubber and tin barons. The carefully restored shop fronts on *Krabi Road* at the corner of Satun Road and the large Taoist temple *Bang Niaw (Phuket Road)* speak to the affluence of the residents back in the day.

WAT CHALONG

Another Buddhist temple you may think – but Wat Chalong is not just any old temple! It is Phuket's largest and busiest wat, attracting busloads of tourists and Thais especially on festive holidays when Buddhism and superstition are celebrated with plenty of fireworks, fortune telling sticks and gold-leaf paper. *Daily 6am–5pm | free admission | Chalong | 8 km (5 miles) south of Phuket Town, accessible via national road 4021*

FOOD & DRINK

INSIDER TIP CHINA INN CAFE

Regulars to Phuket swear by this café – a bright-green oasis where you can restore your energy level in the hustle and bustle of Phuket Town. Thai cuisine and cappuccino taste especially good in this beautifully restored town house with a courtyard. *Tue, Wed, Sun 10.30am–6.30pm, Thu–Sat 10.30am–9pm | 20 Thalang Rd | mobile tel. 08 19 79 82 58 | Moderate*

INSIDER TIP INDY NIGHT MARKET

This colourful night market in Phuket Town is full of tempting smells and a popular hotspot for Phuket's young people: outdoor bars with live music, street food, smoothies and excellent array of stalls selling fashion jewellery, flip-flops and lots of trinkets. *Wed–Fri 4pm–10.30pm | New Dibuk Rd/Limelight Av.*

MOM TRI'S KITCHEN ↯

High above the sea between Kata and Kata Noi, a delicious combination of Thai and Mediterranean fare is served. *12 Kata Noi Rd | tel. 0 76 33 35 68 | www.momtri phuket.com | Expensive*

SHOPPING

The largest shopping centre on the island is the *Jungceylon (www.jungceylon. com)* at Patong Beach, complete with a department store and many smaller shops and restaurants. Another large plaza, the *Central Festival (www.central festivalphuket.com)* lies on the road from Phuket Town to Patong.

BEACHES

The most developed beach on Phuket is *Patong Beach.* With all its big hotels, however, it is also really crowded. *Karon* and *Kata* beaches are slightly less busy, while the beaches of *Ao Sane, Bang Tao, Kamala, Karon Noi, Kata Noi, Nai Harn, Nai Yang, Naithon, Pansea* and *Surin* are relatively quiet.

SPORTS & ACTIVITIES

From kayak tours, wakeboarding, parasailing high above the water to the dangerous jetskis: all kinds of watersports are available on Phuket. The island is the centre of Thailand's diving tourism, since the water quality in the Andaman Sea is generally better than that of the Gulf of Thailand (links for diving spots can be found at *www.phuket.*

From outside, you wouldn't guess there are so many festivities at Wat Chalong

com/diving). You can also climb or fly through the treetops on ziplines at *Flying Hanuman (Kathu | tel. 0 76 32 32 64 | www.flyinghanuman.com)* or go for a bungee jump with *Jungle Bungy Jump (Kathu | tel. 0 76 32 13 51 | www.phuket bungy.com)* More meditative options include mini-golf (Patong, Kata), golf (several courses), shooting and riding (Chalong).

ENTERTAINMENT

With its countless bars, Patong Beach is the stronghold of the island's nightlife. Opulent transvestite shows are the main event at *Phuket Simon Cabaret (430–900 baht | www.phuket-simon cabaret.com)*. A classy disco is *Seduction (www.seductiondisco.com)*. The gigantic theme park *FantaSea (admission from 1800 baht, long queues! | www.phuket-fantasea.com)* on Kamala Beach is a top attraction with its magical costume extravaganza. The folklore show with its museum village in *Siam Niramit Phuket (admission from 1500 baht | Chalermp-rakiet Rd (Bypass Rd) | www.siamniramit. com)* is rather bombastic and maybe not to everyone's taste. You can listen to good live music at the very popular *Timber Hut (118 Yaowaraj Rd)* in Phuket Town.

KA JOK SEE

Let's eat and party – at Khun Lek and his dancing waiters in this iconic establishment. The all-you-can-eat Thai buffet is excellent but once the tables are cleared this century-old villa transforms into a crazy nightclub with a kind of group happening complete with extravagant cabaret, champagne, red roses, transvestites and other surprises – and the fun really starts when the guests start dancing on the tables. All this fun comes at a price so be prepared to pay at least 2000 baht per head. Book in advance. *Phuket Town | 26 Takua Pa Rd | tel. 0 76 21 79 03 | Expensive*

WHERE TO STAY

INSIDER TIP BAIPHO

This boutique hotel is a gem – it feels like staying at an art gallery. Each of the comfortable rooms styled by Swiss fashion photographer Rudi Horber (who died in 2017) is a work of art. The beach is only a stone's throw away. *19 rooms | Patong | 205/2–13 Rat Utit 200 Pee Rd | by Hotel Montana Grand | tel. 0 76 29 20 74 | www.baipho.com | Budget–Expensive*

FANTASY HILL BUNGALOWS

These peaceful, friendly and very affordable bungalows lie on the hill between the Kata and Karon beaches. It is only a ten minute's walk from Fantasy Hill to both of them. The spacious rooms and bungalows are furnished in Thai style. *34 rooms | 8/1 Karon Rd | tel. 0 76 33 01 06 | sites.google.com/site/fantasyhillbungalow | Budget*

ROYAL PHUKET CITY

Begin exploring the island from the best hotel in the city. It is definitely a better value for money than the places at the beach. It features a pool, gym, sauna and spa plus a café with a cake shop. *251 rooms | Phuket Town | Phang Nga Rd | close to the centre | tel. 0 76 23 33 33 | www.royalphuketcity.com | Moderate–Expensive*

TWINPALMS PHUKET

Elegant, yet sober architecture and luxurious rooms, some of which have their own private pool, from which you can swim into the big pool. But of course, amenities such as the "beach butler", the beautiful water garden and the hotel's own, trendy INSIDER TIP *Catch Beach Club (www.catchbeachclub.com)* come with a price tag. *97 rooms | Surin Beach | tel. 0 76 31 65 00 | www.twinpalms-phuket.com | Expensive*

INFORMATION

TOURISM AUTHORITY OF THAILAND
Phuket Town | 191 Thalang Rd | tel. 0 76 21 10 36

WHERE TO GO

KO PHI PHI ★
(136 C6) *(ɯ B16)*

A jungle mountain in the azure blue sea, towering limestone cliffs and glorious white beaches greet you to Phi Phi. A picture-book place you long to visit. Its beauty is best appreciated from above when you have climbed to the ⚘ *viewpoint* 200 m/656 ft above sea level and have gazed over the stunning main beaches of *Lo Dalam* and *Ton Sai.* On the beaches below, you can enjoy your days sunbathing, experience flash storms at sunset and party all night entertained by fire shows.

This 24x7 fiesta was interrupted abruptly only once: The 2004 tsunami destroyed the island village, but it has since been rebuilt; bungalows, pubs, shops, dive shops and the party mile are in demand as never before, which is fatal for the environment. In season, Phi Phi attracts many daytrippers from Phuket and Krabi. who sail in on a whole armada of ferries, cutters, longtail boats and yachts in a kind of regatta. But seriously, anyone who wants to see and get the most out of Phi Phi has unfortunately arrived a few decades too late and is forced to share the island's beauty with thousands of other tourists from around the world. They flock to the village on main island of *Phi Phi Don* to snorkel in the crystal clear water and take in the splendour of untouched *Phi Phi Le,* the small neigh-

Best snorkelling conditions in the crystal clear water off Ko Phi Phi

bouring island where Leonardo Di Caprio trudged through the powdered sand of enchanted *Maya Bay* in the film "The Beach", which by the way did not carry a 400 baht (around £ 10/$ 12.50) admission charge in those days. For years, environmentalists and scientists have been demanding that Maya Bay should be closed to tourists during the off-season for nature to recover. This measure was finally adopted for the first time in 2018 and it remains to be seen whether it will be repeated again in the future.

There are plenty of rooms on Ko Phi Phi, but not the best value for money. For a more economic alternative, try *Papaya Phi Phi Resort (36 rooms | Ton Sai | 262 Moo 7 | tel. 075 81 87 30 | www. papayaphiphi.com | Moderate)* for a comfortable stay.

PHANG NGA BAY ★
(136 C5) (*Ⓜ B15*)
Bizarrely-shaped limestone islands and islets jut out of the sea to heights of up to 300 m (1,000 ft) where the waters are awash with islands in all shapes and sizes. The most famous is *James Bond Island (Ko Tapu)* which featured in "The Man with the Golden Gun" filmed in 1974. 007 returned to Phang Nga Bay in 1997 when the bay served as a double for Ha Long Bay in Vietnam for the film "Tomorrow Never Dies". The bay is a protected marine national park where you can also visit the often overcrowded stilted Muslim village of *Ko Panyi*.

Souvenirs are again available at every turn. The best way to immerse yourself in the region's beauty is by canoe on a tour into the *hongs,* which are hidden behind the island's high mountains and can only be viewed from the air: a circular lagoon world with turquoise waters and mangrove forest – magnificent and enigmatic scenery which resembles the setting of a fantasy film. Only insiders, such as the tour guides, know when the tides are low enough to enter these "Open Sesame" jewels through underground stalactite caves, resembling natural tunnels. They only remain accessible for a few hours before the tide rises and closes the caves' entrance as if by magic. Every tour operator organises tours into this stunning bay (see p. 106). *Admission 300 baht*

DISCOVERY TOURS

1

THAILAND AT A GLANCE

START: ① Phuket Town
END: ⑬ Sop Ruak

19 days
Driving time
(without stops)
50 hours

Distance:
🚗 2,800 km/1,740 miles

COSTS: approx. 96,000 baht for 2 people (accommodation, food & drink, rental car, petrol and guided excursions)
WHAT TO PACK: navigation system or smartphone with GPS, swim gear, sun protection and mosquito repellent/nets

      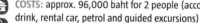 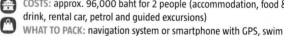 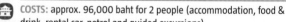

Experience the many different facets of Thailand on this cleverly devised route. Leaving touristy Phuket behind, you'll visit breathtaking natural highlights,

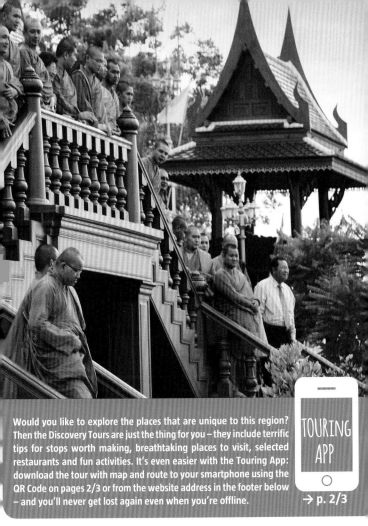

Would you like to explore the places that are unique to this region? Then the Discovery Tours are just the thing for you – they include terrific tips for stops worth making, breathtaking places to visit, selected restaurants and fun activities. It's even easier with the Touring App: download the tour with map and route to your smartphone using the QR Code on pages 2/3 or from the website address in the footer below – and you'll never get lost again even when you're offline.

TOURING APP

→ p. 2/3

amazing beaches and a royal residence before coming to the metropolis of Bangkok with the royal palace and the best shopping in all of Southeast Asia. Travel through former royal cities further to the north of the country where charming temples and spectacular mountain ranges will cast you under their spell.

Your tour begins with two days on ❶ Phuket → p. 87. Thailand's most beloved holiday island not only has an international airport serviced by all the major car rental agencies, but also a dozen amazing beaches. After explor-

DAY 1–2
❶ Phuket

DAY 3–4

133 km/82.5 mi

2 Phang Nga Bay

178 km/111 mi

3 Khao Sok National Park

DAY 5–7

221 km/137 mi

4 Ko Samui

DAY 8

647 km/402 mi

5 Hua Hin

DAY 9–11

192 km/119 mi

6 Bangkok

ing the fascinating old centre of **Phuket Town** with its Chinese temples and old Sino-Portuguese style villas, **drive south to the impressive** Big Buddha. Afterwards, spend a relaxing day at the **beach of Patong** before attending a transvestite show at the **Phuket Simon Cabaret**. Spend both nights at the artsy boutique hotel **Baipho**.

On the third day, take National Road 402 and Hwy 4 to Phang Nga on the mainland. At **2** Phang Nga Bay → p. 91, embark on a boat excursion to the imposing rock islands that even left an impression on James Bond. Once you've docked, **follow highways 4, 415 and 401 into the jungle of 3** Khao Sok National Park → p. 78. Check into the beautifully-situated **Khaosok Rainforest Resort** *(28 rooms | tel. 0 77 39 51 35 | Budget–Moderate)*, where you will spend a total of two nights. The next morning, take off on a hiking tour through the jungle for the day.

Day 5 begins with a **drive along National Road 401 to Don Sak harbour to catch the car ferry over to 4** Ko Samui → p. 80. Enjoy all the comforts of **The Waterfront** hotel *(18 rooms | tel. 0 77 42 71 65 | www.thewaterfrontbophut.com | Moderate)* for three nights. This little hotel sits directly on Bo Phut Beach. **The ring road around the island will take you to all the beaches.** Make sure to light a few incense sticks at the **Big Buddha** and stroll through the magical **Secret Buddha Garden**. First and foremost, take time to unwind and clear the cobwebs from your head.

On the eighth day of the tour, **take the first ferry back to the mainland and drive the long stretch north along Route 4 to the seaside resort of 5** Hua Hin (pop. 80,000). The seafood restaurants right on the water more than make up for the rather strenuous drive with fish fresh from the grill. All the charm of the 1920s awaits you in the luxurious **Centara Grand Beach Resort** *(249 rooms | 1 Damnernkasem Road | tel. 0 32 51 20 21 | www.centarahotelsresorts.com | Expensive)*.

The tour continues along Route 4 and National Road 35 on the ninth day, bringing you to Thailand's vibrant capital, **6** Bangkok → p. 35. Leave your rental car at your stylish accommodation **Ariyasomvilla** and explore the metropolis for three days **using public transport.** The fabulous **Grand Palace** and the **Wat Pho** are absolute musts-sees for anyone visiting the capital. You can shop till you drop in the area around the Skytrain station Siam. If you happen to be in Bangkok at the weekend, you should definitely plan to walk over the gigantic **Chatuchak Weekend Market**.

Leave Bangkok on Hwy 1 heading north to your first stop on day 12, the old royal city of **⑦ Ayutthaya → p. 32**, which is only about one and a half hours away. This historic city is dotted with the ruins of temples and palaces – it is particularly enchanting at night when it is lit up by spotlights. After spending the night in the large **Kantary Hotel**, head out the next day **further north, following Hwy 32 first and then Hwys 11 and 12 over the broad Menam plain, the rice bowl of the country, to ⑧ Sukhothai → p. 44**. In the capital of the first Thai empire, **Old Sukhothai**, around 200 ruins in the historic park attest to the former glory of the "dawn of happiness" as this temple city was called when it was founded in 1238. The charming **Ruean Thai Hotel** will be your home for two nights.

On day 15, **take National Road 101 and Hwy 11 to ⑨ Chiang Mai → p. 46**, where you will stay for two nights in the attractive **Baan Hanibah B & B** in the heart of the quite impressive old city centre. For a lovely day trip, **follow Hwy 108 to the west, then drive up the serpentine National Road 1009 up to ⑩ Doi Inthanon → p. 50**, the highest mountain in Thailand at a height of 2,565 m (8,415 ft). Go for a small hike through the cloud forest near the summit.

Depart Chiang Mai on day 17 and drive along Hwy 118 further to ⑪ Chiang Rai → p. 51. Members of the mountain tribes sell handicrafts and perform dances on the **night market** in the city. A visit to the spectacular "white temple" **Wat Rong Khun** must be on your agenda if you're visiting Chiang Rai. Spend the last two nights of your tour in luxury at **The Legend Resort**. If at all possible, you should definitely take a little trip **via**

DAY 12–14

130 km / 81 mi

⑦ Ayutthaya

388 km / 241 mi

⑧ Sukhothai

DAY 15–16

322 km / 200 mi

⑨ Chiang Mai

107 km / 66 mi

⑩ Doi Inthanon

DAY 17–19

298 km / 185 mi

⑪ Chiang Rai

100 km/62 mi

⑫ Mae Salong

78 km/48 mi

⑬ Sop Ruak

Hwy 1 and National Road 1089 into the mountains to the village of ⑫ Mae Salong → p. 51. Descendants of Chinese Kuomintag soldiers now cultivate coffee and tea here. Walk through the village and enjoy its truly unique atmosphere. After that, follow in the tracks of the drug lords who once ruled over the Golden Triangle: **The National Roads 1130, 1016 and 1290 lead you to ⑬ Sop Ruak → p. 52** and to the great **Hall of Opium** museum. Countless shops and market stalls line both banks of the Mekong. After returning to Chiang Rai, you can catch a plane at the airport back to Bangkok or to another destination in Thailand.

2 ACTIVELY EXPLORING ANCIENT KINGDOMS

START: ① Chiang Mai	7 days
END: ⑪ Umphang	Driving time
	(without stops)
Distance:	15 hours
➡ 785 km/488 miles	

COSTS: approx. 32,500 baht for 2 people (accommodation, food & drink, rental car, petrol and guided excursions)

WHAT TO PACK: navigation system or smartphone with GPS, swim gear and sun protection

Follow the traces of ancient kingdoms and explore the rugged mountains on the border to Myanmar on this route leading south from Chiang Mai. You'll encounter sweet-tempered elephants, ride in a horse-drawn carriage and keep fit with mountain bike and rafting adventures.

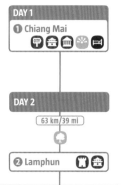

DAY 1

① Chiang Mai

The starting point for this tour is ① **Chiang Mai → p. 46**, where you will check into **The 3 Sis**. Visit the impressive temple buildings in the old city centre as well as the interesting history museums. Explore the **Wat Phra That Doi Suthep** situated beautifully above the city at your leisure.

DAY 2

63 km/39 mi

② Lamphun

On **Hwy 106 to the south**, you will drive through a lovely avenue lined by old jungle trees, some of which have grown to a height of 40 m (130 ft), to get to ② **Lamphun** (pop. 14,000). The city was once the official residence of the rulers of the legendary kingdom of Haripunchai. The ruins of the old city walls and the beautiful **Wat Phra That Haripunchai** attest to its long history. **In less than a half hour's drive on Hwy 11 towards Lampang, you will come to the road that branches off to the ❸ Thai Elephant Conservation Center →** p. 110. Watch one of the elephant shows and maybe even help wash one of the thick-skinned giants. You can also visit the elephant museum, kindergarten and hospital.

Return to Hwy 11 and drive to the busy, yet pleasant provincial capital of ❹ Lampang (pop. 60,000). Hop onto one of the colourful horse-drawn carriages for a tour around the city *(200–300 baht)* and stop at some of the

44 km/27 mi

❸ Thai Elephant Conservation Center

33 km/20 mi

❹ Lampang

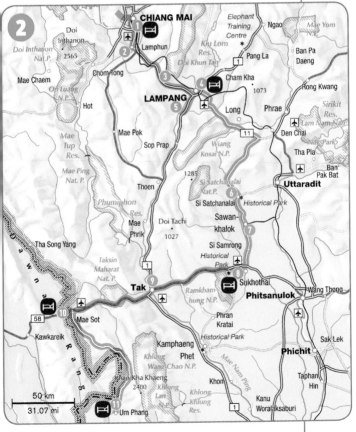

97

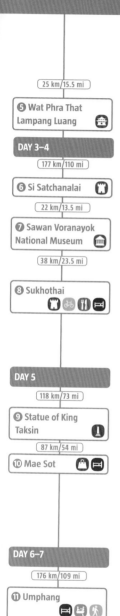

25 km / 15.5 mi

❺ Wat Phra That Lampang Luang

DAY 3–4

177 km / 110 mi

❻ Si Satchanalai

22 km / 13.5 mi

❼ Sawan Voranayok National Museum

38 km / 23.5 mi

❽ Sukhothai

DAY 5

118 km / 73 mi

❾ Statue of King Taksin

87 km / 54 mi

❿ Mae Sot

DAY 6–7

176 km / 109 mi

⓫ Umphang

lively markets, stately temples and teak houses such as the **Baan Sao Nak** (Ratwattana Rd | admission 50 baht). A special flair and personal service await you at **Auangkham Resort** (14 rooms | 51 Wang Nua Rd | tel. 0 54 22 13 06 | www.auangkhamlampang.com | Budget). If you have time, make the worthwhile trip **to the southwest via Hwy 1 and National Road 1034** to ❺ INSIDER TIP **Wat Phra That Lampang Luang** (daily 7.30am–5pm | free admission), perhaps the most enthralling temple in northern Thailand.

On the third day, **Hwy 11 will lead you through rice paddies to the southeast to the junction with Route 101. Turn right towards Sukhothai.** At the historic park of ❻ **Si Satchanalai** (daily 8am–5pm | admission 100 baht), temple ruins tell the story of the city's past. **On the way, stop in Sawankhalok** to see the unique ceramic pieces at the ❼ **Sawanworanayok National Museum** (Wed–Sun 9am–4pm | admission 50 baht). Continue on to ❽ **Sukhothai** → p. 44. Not only does **Old Sukhothai** also have an impressive historical park, but it is situated within an authentic rural setting. Explore the area on your fourth day on a guided mountain bike tour through the rice paddies and villages. The Frenchman Michel offers charming accommodation at **Lotus Village** (20 rooms | 170 Rajthanee Rd | tel. 0 55 62 14 84 | www.lotus-village.com | Budget) and a warm Thai meal awaits in the popular restaurant **Rom Pho**.

Continue westward on Hwy 12 and look to the mountains in the distance. Several roads converge in Tak (pop. 25,000), which has little to offer other than the ❾ **Statue of King Taksin** (1734–82) who was born here. After a short break, **keep driving on the curvy Hwy 105 through the mountains to** ❿ **Mae Sot** (pop. 55,000). Many of the shops glisten and shine because this multicultural city on the border to Myanmar is a centre of the gemstone trade. Visit the colourful **market** at the end of Hwy 105, directly on the river Moei that marks the border to Myanmar. For a simple, but clean and centrally-located accommodation, check into the **J2 Hotel** (45 rooms | 149/8 Intarakeeree Rd | tel. 0 55 54 69 99 | Budget).

The next morning, it's time for the long drive **on National Road 1090** to the isolated ⓫ **Umphang** region. Spend the night at **Tu Ka Su Cottage** (30 rooms | west of the bridge | tel. 0 55 56 12 95 | www.tukasu.webs.com | Budget) and book a rafting or trekking tour for your last day on this route.

3 ADVENTURES IN THE JUNGLE OF THE GIGANTIC FLOWER

START: ❶ Phuket END: ❶ Phuket	3 days Driving time (without stops) 9 hours
Distance: 🔄 512 km/318 miles	

COSTS: approx. 9600–10,700 baht for 2 people (rental car from 900 baht/day, petrol 1150 baht, accommodation 1780 baht/night, National Park admission 180 baht/day, jungle tours 430–610 baht, tubing 320 baht/hour and canoe tours 610 baht for 2 hours)

WHAT TO PACK: navigation system or smartphone with GPS, sun protection, mosquito repellent/nets, swim gear and a change of clothes

Together with the surrounding conservation areas, the Khao Sok National Park is the largest jungle area in southern Thailand. Explore this "evergreen" paradise on foot and by canoe.

As soon as you drive away from Phuket, there will be no doubt in your mind that this route is heading into the jungle – with a view of the blue ocean to boot. Leave ❶ Phuket → p. 87 **on Hwy 402 North. At the junction**

DAY 1

❶ Phuket

Hike through the jungle on the trails in Khao Sok National Park

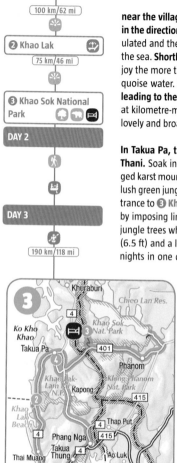

100 km/62 mi

② Khao Lak

75 km/46 mi

③ Khao Sok National Park

DAY 2

DAY 3

190 km/118 mi

near the village of Khok Kloi, turn onto Hwy 4 and drive in the direction of Takua Pa. This area is only sparsely populated and the green jungle mountains spread almost to the sea. **Shortly before you come to Khao Lak**, you can enjoy the more than impressive view of the glimmering turquoise water. **Little roads branch off from the highway, leading to the beaches of ② Khao Lak → p. 74.** The road at kilometre-marker 60, for example, will take you to the lovely and broad Nang Thong Beach.

In Takua Pa, turn onto Hwy 401 heading towards Surat Thani. Soak in the spectacular landscape with huge, rugged karst mountains that rise up almost vertically from the lush green jungle. In the afternoon you will arrive at the entrance to **③ Khao Sok National Park → p. 78.** Surrounded by imposing limestone cliffs, the park is home to gigantic jungle trees whose buttress roots jut up over 2 metres tall (6.5 ft) and a large variety of animals. Sleep the next few nights in one of the romantic tree houses at **INSIDER TIP Our Jungle House** (12 rooms | mobile tel. 08 14 17 05 46 | www.khaosokaccommo dation.com | Moderate).

After a good night's sleep, head off into the park. It is easy to hike on your own if you **follow the marked trails.** The half-day jungle tours that you can book through the resorts and travel agencies also come well-recommended. The guides will lead you to waterfalls a bit further away and they know where to find the Rafflesia, which bear the largest flowers in the world. In the afternoon, head out on the water. Book a tubing excursion at your hotel and sail down the Sok River on your donut-shaped raft.

Begin the last day with a half-day canoe trip to the **Chiew Lan (Ratchaprapha)** reservoir with its steep limestone cliffs and enchanting caves. You can book this adventure tour at your hotel as well. Afterwards, it's time to hit the road again. **Drive west on Hwy 401, and turn left in Takua Pa onto National Road 4032. A bit to the south of the village, you will** come across a real gem: the somewhat hidden ❹ **old town of Takua Pa** → p. 77 where many aged Chinese storefronts still tell of the great era of the pewter boom in the 19th century. After a stroll, **follow National Roads 4032 and 4090 towards Phang Nga and then take Hwys 4 and 402 to return to** ❶ **Phuket** → p. 87.

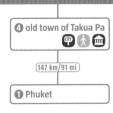

❹ old town of Takua Pa

147 km / 91 mi

❶ Phuket

---

4 SUN, SAND AND FUN FOR THE WHOLE FAMILY

START: ❶ Bangkok END: ❼ Trat	9 days Driving time (without stops) 12 hours
Distance: 🚗 640 km/400 miles	

COSTS: approx. 64,000 baht for a family of four (accommodation, food & drink, rental car, petrol, admission fees and excursions)
WHAT TO PACK: swim gear and sun protection

Thailand's east coast is perfect for a family-friendly tour with lots of variety using public transport. Start in Bangkok and follow along the 400-km long (250 miles) Sukhumvit Highway (Hwy 3) almost all the way to the border with Cambodia.

From ❶ **Bangkok** → p. 35, take a taxi **to the southeast on the Sukhumvit Highway** to get to the world's largest outdoor museum, ❷ **Ancient Siam** (daily 9am–7pm | www.ancientcitygroup.net/ancientsiam). On a rental bike or a golf cart, you can explore "all of Thailand" in one day as replicas of over 100 attractions are dotted around the sprawling museum grounds. Afterwards, return to **your waiting taxi and take Hwy 3 directly to** ❸ **Pattaya** → p. 69. The somewhat strange world of **Ripley's Believe It Or Not** is quite an experience for families with children. If you are interested in culture, head to the beautiful teak wood **Sanctuary of Truth**. The popular **Thai Garden Resort** is a good place to book a room for the night

The next day is all about adventure with a zip line course. At **Flight of the Gibbon** (www.treetopasia.com), you can swing from tree to tree on steel cables. Once you have

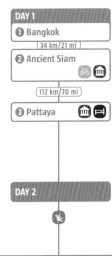

DAY 1

❶ Bangkok

34 km / 21 mi

❷ Ancient Siam

112 km / 70 mi

❸ Pattaya

DAY 2

overcome your initial hesitation, you can enjoy a full adrenaline rush. A visit to the adjacent **Khao Kheow Open Zoo** is just the thing afterwards.

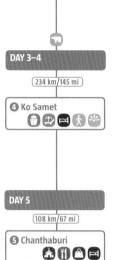

DAY 3–4

234 km/145 mi

❹ Ko Samet

Your next destination is the island of ❹ **Ko Samet** → p. 73. Spend two relaxing days at the pleasant **Vongduean Resort** situated directly on a fine sand beach. With the minibus from Malibu Travel *(tel. 0 38 37 02 59 | www.malibu-travel.com)*, **travel along the coast on Hwy 3 to Ban Phe, and cross over to the island with the resort's own ferry.** Just a ten minute walk from the resort will bring you to a **INSIDERTIP** fabulous place to watch the sunset. **Go through the entrance towards the street and follow the "sunset" signs to the cliffs on the other side of the island.**

DAY 5

108 km/67 mi

❺ Chanthaburi

Take the midday ferry back to the mainland and drive with a pre-chartered taxi along Hwy 3 to the charming town of ❺ **Chanthaburi** → p. 73, which is home to Thailand's largest cathedral, **Notre-Dame**. Don't miss out on the restaurant **Chanthorn Phochana** *(102/5–8 Benjamarachuthid Rd | tel. 0 39 30 23 50 | Budget)*, which dishes up the local speciality **INSIDERTIP** *Bai Cha Moung*, a tasty and rich herb soup. The town owes its wealth to its sapphire and ruby trade that is apparently a quite profitable business. Visit the **Chantaburi Gem & Jewelry Center**

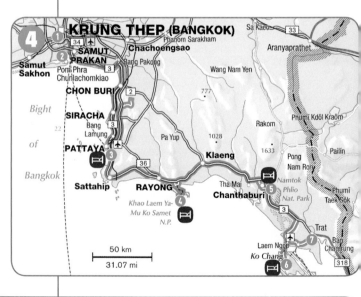

Sun, sea, sand and palm trees are just what the doctor ordered on Ko Chang

(daily 8am–7pm | Sri Chan Rd) to admire the gemstones and jewellery. Book one of the comfortable, yet functional rooms at **Kasemsarn Hotel** *(60 rooms | 98/1 Benjamarachuthid Rd | tel. 03931 2340 | www.hotelkasemsarn. com | Budget)* for the night.

The next morning, take a **taxi along Hwy 3 and National Road 3156 to get to the ferry station Ao Thammachat near Trat. Ferries depart regularly for the hour-long trip to the island of ⑥ Ko Chang → p. 64.** Settle into your room at **Klong Prao Resort** and hit the beach with the same name for a good dose of relaxing sun and sea. On the last two days on the island, gear up once again for a bit more activity. Book a kayak tour with Kayak Chang *(Klong Prao Beach | at Amari Emerald Cove Resort | www. kayakchang.com)* and a cruise through the archipelago with Thaifun Day-Cruise *(mobile tel. 0810 03 48 00 | www. thaifun-kohchang.com).* On your ninth day, **return to the mainland and take a taxi to ⑦ Trat** where you can catch a flight back to Bangkok.

DAY 6–9

88 km/54.5 mi

⑥ Ko Chang

67 km/41.5 mi

⑦ Trat

SPORTS & ACTIVITIES

Not content just to lie on the beach? Then go for a dive or a climb. Are you looking for relaxation? Give your mind a rest while practicing yoga, or treat yourself to a Thai massage.

BALLOON RIDES

Want to experience Thailand from above? No problem: you'll find information on hot air balloon rides at *www.balloonadventurethailand.com/index*.

DIVING

The best dive sites are located in the Andaman Sea in the waters around Phuket and Khao Lak; the uninhabited ⭐ *Similan Islands* 50 km (31 miles) west of Khao Lak rank among the world's top diving destinations, but also around the Phi Phi Islands and down the coast to the Malaysian border a colourful underwater world awaits the diver. The premier dive sites in the Gulf of Thailand are around the small island Ko Tao north of Ko Samui, but there are also great sites off Pattaya and Ko Chang. A one-day excursion with two dives costs approx. 2900 baht; a three- to four-day basic course starts at 7100 baht. For detailed information on dive sites, seasons, etc, visit: *www.divetheworldthailand.com*

GOLF

Golf courses are plentiful in Thailand. Top destinations are Pattaya with

From trekking and diving to massages and yoga – Thailand offers everything from thrilling adventures to relaxing spa days

around a dozen courses and Phuket with seven courses of international standard, but there are also courses in Bangkok, Kanchanaburi, Chiang Mai, Hua Hin, at Khao Yai National Park and on Ko Samui. You can request a golf brochure from the Tourism Authority of Thailand. *www.golf orient.com*

HORSE TREKKING

Boris Mimietz and his attentive team at the *Thai Horse Farm (Phrao | 100 km* *(62 miles) north of Chiang Mai | mobile tel. 08 69 19 38 46 | www.thaihorsefarm. com)* will lead you through the *Sri Lanna National Park* atop Asian mountain horses. The tours in small groups are suitable for beginners who have never before sat on a horse, making for a stress-free adventure off the beaten tourist track. For a one-day tour including food and transport to and from Chiang Mai as well as all the necessary equipment, you will pay approx 4600 baht; four nights with full board cost 23,500 baht.

MASSAGES & WELLBEING

If you have a preconceived notion of what a Thai massage involves, then you'll be surprised when you're given a pair of baggy pyjamas to wear. *Raksaa thaang nuad (also known as nuat phaen boran)* is a tradition stretching back 2500 years and uses no oils. The classic (!) Thai massage involves compressing, pulling, stretching and rocking the body to stimulate the body's main meridians. The elbows, knees and even the feet of the masseurs are used for this. "Lazy man's yoga" is how the Thais jokingly refer to this type of massage. Some of the 51 techniques used are in fact controversial especially if they are performed by an inadequately trained masseurs wo lack the necessary medical and physiological expertise and are not familiar with the client's history of health and his language. The Thai-equivalent of the Red Cross advises against performing on older people the technique of applying pressure to the groin's main artery for minutes and then the traditional (and, in the worst case scenario, final) tug of the head to end the full-body massage. If a Thai massage sounds too strenuous, you can treat yourself instead to a Swedish oil massage or even a four-handed massage. The choice of wellness and massage treatments ranges from luxury spas and inexpensive massage studios to traditional healers. It's good to be aware that the women offering massages on the beach *(approx. 320 baht)* have not been professionally trained, for example at the prestigious *Wat Pho Massage School* (see p. 37) in Bangkok. They usually have only undergone rudimentary training.

ROCK CLIMBING

Rock climbers from all over the world test their skills on the limestone cliffs at the beaches of Railay and Ton Sai in Krabi as well as on Ko Phi Phi and are rewarded with spectacular views over the coast and the sea. Chiang Mai also has some good climbs. Introductory course 780–1,200 baht. *www.thailandclimbing. com, www.rockclimbing-thailand.info*

SAILING

With its beautiful islands, the Andaman Sea is an eldorado for sailors. But you can also set sail in the Gulf of Thailand (Pattaya, Ko Chang, Ko Samui). The list of charter companies in Thailand is virtually endless. *www.yachtcharterthailand. com*

SEA CANOE TOURS

The limestone cliffs of Phang Nga Bay provide a stunning backdrop for a canoeing trip. There are day trips from Phuket from around 3500 baht as well as tours lasting three days with overnight stays on the accompanying boat or in tents on the beach for around 25,000 baht, e.g. with *John Gray's Sea Canoe (tel. 0 76 25 45 05 | www.johngray-seacanoe. com)*. Holidaymakers on Ko Samui can paddle through the islands of the National Maritime Park, Ang Thong, e.g. with *Blue Stars Sea Kayaking (tel. 0 77 30 06 15 | www.bluestars.info)*. Bookings can also be made through local travel agencies.

TREKKING

Could you go three days without Internet, hot water or hairdryer? If yes, then pack your hiking boots! Hiking through the forested mountains of the North is a fantastic experience. But even more interesting for many tourists is the chance to come into contact with the mountain tribes that cling to their traditions in isolated villages. The centre of trekking tourism is Chiang Mai, but from there it's several hours drive before you get into any real mountains. If you start your ⭐ trekking adventure in Pai or in Mae Hong Son, you are already among the mountains. Most tours also include an elephant ride and bamboo rafting. A three-day tour for six people will cost from 1800 baht each. It's advisable to use only travel agencies that are registered with the Tourism Authority of Thailand. *www.dnp.go.th*

WHITE-WATER RAFTING

The INSIDERTIP *Umphang Jungle,* 170 km (105 miles) south of Mae Sot in the Thailand/Myanmar border region, is considered the most virgin area of tropical rainforest in the country. The Mae Klong River winds its way through the wilderness, sometimes at a leisurely pace, sometimes churning over rapids and ending in the multi-level *Thi Lo Su,* Thailand's largest waterfall. Several operators in Mae Sot and Umphang offer rafting tours, e.g. *Umphangburi Resort (tel. 0 55 56 15 76 | www.umphang buriresort.com).* To get there, you need to take the last off-road adventure in Thailand — yet a tarmac road was already under construction at the time of going to print. A four-day tour (min. 2 people) costs approx. 10,700 baht per person. Adventurous rafting tours are also offered on the Pai River near the town of Pai from June to January.

YOGA

A vacation for body and soul: yoga and meditation are offered at several retreats. The island of ● *Ko Phangan* in particular has developed as a spiritual centre for those who want to explore their inner selves. Addresses and links: *www.thaiwebsites.com/yoga.asp.*

Trekking tour near Mae Hong Son

TRAVEL WITH KIDS

Travellers with children are warmly welcomed everywhere. Don't be surprised to see Thais pat your children on the head or take them by the hand.

The joy Thais display towards children of *farang* is genuine. Especially in smaller hotels and resorts, little guests are often treated like family, and staff may occasionally even volunteer to fill in as a babysitters. Economically-priced rooms in particular are often furnished with three beds or a double and a single bed; an additional bed can be supplied on request. You can buy baby food and nappies at supermarkets in the tourist centres and larger towns. It's advisable to leave your buggy at home though: pavements – if there are any – are not usually in the best state of repair, and progress can be

torture, especially if they're blocked by souvenir stalls. A more practical option is a baby or child carrier for your back or chest.

CENTRAL THAILAND

CHILDREN'S DISCOVERY MUSEUM
(131 D5) (ω D9)

Learning is fun at this museum with oversized Lego bricks for little constructors, dinosaur bones in the sandpit and a fire station. Creating giant soapy bubbles or crawling through the tunnel of mirrors are also popular attractions. There are also painting and handicraft workshops, a shady playground with climbing walls, ropes and slides and a small water park with water cannons and foun-

A kingdom for kids: children are welcome in Thailand. And exciting adventures are around every corner

tains (don't forget to bring a change of clothes for the kids). And the best news is that admission is free! *Tue–Sun 10am–4pm | Soi 4 Kamphaeng Phet Rd | Queen Sirikit Park | Chatuchak | Bangkok | short. travel/tai12*

DREAM WORLD (131 D5) (*ᗡ D9*)

A huge theme park featuring a nostalgic train, Wonderful Garden, Fairy Tale Land, Snow World, water park and Hollywood Action shows. *Mon–Fri 10am–5pm, Sat, Sun 10am–7pm | admission from 1200 baht, free for children shorter than 90 cm | 62 Rangsit-Ongkarak Rd | Rangsit | approx. 10 minutes' drive north of Don Muang Airport | www.dreamworld. co.th/en*

KIDZANIA BANGKOK (U D4) (*ᗡ d4*)

A miniature city planned down to the last detail where kids can try out all kids of jobs and professions. Among the more than 80 different choices, there are dream jobs such as firefighter, pilot or doctor as well as more unusual ones including sushi chef, secret agent or forensics expert. Everything is sponsored by big-name companies, which means that little mechanics work on Toyota cars and Coca-Cola bottles have to be filled. Be prepared for long queues and it's best to go in a group because most of the visitors are Thai children who don't speak English – but you can always use sign language and the fun factor is guaranteed. *Mon–Fri 10am–5pm, Sat, Sun 10.30am–8.30pm | admission Mon–Fri 600 baht, children 1000 baht, Sat, Sun 720 baht, children 1200 baht | 991 Rama I Rd | Siam Paragon | 5th floor | Bangkok | bangkok.kidzania.com*

MADAME TUSSAUDS (U D4) (*[map]* d4)
At this offshoot of the world-famous wax museum, kids can look celebrities such as Katy Perry, Beyoncé, Brad Pitt, Spiderman and Cristiano Ronaldo in the eye. *Daily 10am–8pm | admission from 11 years from 990 baht, online from 645 baht | 989 Rama I Rd | Siam Discovery Center | 6th floor | Bangkok | www.madametussauds.com/bangkok*

SEA LIFE BANGKOK OCEAN WORLD ●
(U D4) (*[map]* d4)
Coral fish, manta rays and even penguins call Thailand's largest aquarium home. Kids will be delighted when they walk under the glass tunnel in the middle of the shark tank or through the life-like rain forest. *Daily 10am–8pm | admission 990 baht, children 790 baht | 991 Rama I Rd | in the Siam Paragon shopping centre | Bangkok | www.sealifebangkok.com/en*

THE NORTH

CHIANG MAI ZOO (126 C3) (*[map]* B3)
The stars of this extensive zoo are two pandas. But in Thailand's largest zoo, there are over 400 other species such as Thai elephants, African giraffes and Australian koala bears. Watch the sharks and small fish at the adjacent aquarium. In the *Snow Dome* visitors both large and small can even go sledging on the artificial snow. *Daily 8am–5pm | admission 150 baht, children 100 baht (100/20 baht extra for the panda zone, 150/100 baht for the Snow Dome) | 100 Huay Kaew Rd | www.chiangmaizoo.com*

ELEPHANT CAMPS
Near Chiang Mai there are countless (more or less good) elephant camps where visitors can watch the animals perform tricks, take a ride on one around the camp or scrub the elephants down as they bathe. The most reputable establishments are the *Elephant Nature Park (126 C2) ([map] B3) (day visit including hotel pick-up from 2500 baht | tel. 053272855 | www.elephantnaturepark. com)* north of Chiang Mai and the famous, government-run *Thai Elephant Conservation Center (TECC) (126 C4) ([map] C4) (daily 9am–3.30pm | admission 200 baht, children 100 baht, elephant rides from 500 baht, mahout course from 4000 baht | Hang Chat | km 28–29 on the Hwy. Lampang–Chiang Mai | tel. 054829333 | www.thailandelephant.org)* in the southeast in Lampang. The TECC is the oldest, largest and most renowned institute of its kind in Thailand and includes an onsite elephant hospital, mahout training program, homestay accommodation for tourists and many other services.

EAST COAST

INSIDER TIP ▶ ART IN PARADISE
(134 C3) (*[map]* D10)
Put your hand in the mouth of the White Shark, tiptoe through Egyptian burial chambers or turn into a butterfly – made possible by fun optical tricks and 3D pic-

tures. The popular exhibition in Pattaya is worthwhile not only with kids or on rainy days. Take pff your shoes before entering. *Daily 9am–10.30pm | admission 400 baht, children 200 baht | Pattaya 2nd Rd | Ban Lamung | in the north of the city near the Amari Garden Hotel | www.artinparadise.co*

KHAO KHEOW OPEN ZOO ★
(135 D2) *(ꝒD10)*

This open-air animal sanctuary, which operates under the patronage of the royal family, is recognised for its animal management and operations. Around 8000 animals from hippos and lions to orang-utans live as close to their natural habitat as possible in the expansive jungle park. Night safaris are also organized. In the *Children's Zoo,* numerous baby animals await visitors. *Daily 9am–5pm, night safari 7pm | several tours on offer, also with overnight stay, incl. pickup service from Bangkok or Pattaya | approx. 50 km (31 miles) north of Pattaya | www.khaokheow.zoothailand.org | www.journeytothejungle.com*

THE SOUTH

DINO PARK (136 C6) *(ꝒA–B16)*
For dinosaur fans: This mini golf course features an artificial volcano and encounters with a variety of dinosaur species. As you go round, it's easy to imagine yourself being back in prehistoric times. *Daily 10am–11pm (the volcano glows only when it is dark) | admission 240 baht, children 180 baht | Karon Beach | Phuket | www.dinopark.com*

PARADISE PARK FARM ☙
(137 E3) *(ꝒC14))*

A large park with goats, rabbits, ponies – a giant petting zoo located in the hills above Ko Samui's west coast. It also fea-

In the kingdom of Thailand, the smallest are the greatest

tures a restaurant, pool, terrific view of the coast, and pleasant temperatures. *Daily 10am–6pm | admission 400 baht, children 200 baht | pick-up service available | junction of the ring road at the village of Ban Saket (signposted)*

FESTIVALS & EVENTS

The timing of religious festivals depends on the position of the sun and the moon, so dates vary from year to year. Local festivals can be similarly moveable. The state tourism authority TAT *(www.tourismthailand.org)* compiles festival dates every year. You can also find a good summary at: *www.thaifestivalblogs.com.* The Buddhist calendar begins with the birth of The Enlightened One. The year 2020 A.D. corresponds to the year 2563 after Buddha.

HOLIDAYS & FESTIVALS

JANUARY

Bor Sang Umbrella Festival: The village of Bor Sang near Chiang Mai in Northern Thailand is renowned for its hand-painted paper umbrellas. On a parade, girls in festive costumes present the most beautiful umbrellas.

JANUARY/FEBRUARY

Chinese New Year: New Year in Bangkok's Chinatown and in many other cities is ushered in with a procession of Chinese deities accompanied by colourful lion and dragon dancing. In Phuket a one-week Temple Festival takes place in the monastery of Wat Chalong (by the village of Chalong).

FEBRUAR

Flower Festival: This three-day long colourful fair with a large flower show takes place on the first weekend in February in Chiang Mai. The highlight is the breathtaking parade on Saturday featuring floats artfully decorated with flowers, people in traditional dress and lots of music.

APRIL

★ ● *Songkran:* Thai New Year (13–15 April) is the wildest festival of all, celebrated by throwing water at everybody in sight. Tourists are not exempt. Some of the biggest celebrations (with a big parade) are in Chiang Mai, where festivities actually begin a day early, on 12 April. In Bangkok, the centre of the water fights is the touristy Khao San Road.

MAY

★ *Royal Ploughing Ceremony Day:* Held during the second week in May, this festival marks the beginning of the rice planting season. A colourful procession takes place at the Grand Palace in Bangkok with the royal family in attendance. Grandstand seats can be booked at tourist offices in Bangkok.

SEPTEMBER/OCTOBER

Buffalo racing: Farm hands are the jockeys and water buffaloes are the mounts for this race meeting in Chonburi (between Bangkok and Pattaya).

⭐ ***Vegetarian festival:*** Bizarre festival in Phuket and, on a smaller scale, in Trang (Southern Thailand). Ethnic Chinese Thais work themselves into a trance before skewering needles, hooks, knives and even drills or umbrellas though their flesh. The participants adhere to a strict vegetarian diet during the festival.

NOVEMBER

⭐ ***Loi Kratong:*** The most enchanting festival of the year takes place at full moon in November. Baskets with flowers, incense and burning candles are floated in the water. The most romantic festivities take place in Sukhothai and Ayutthaya as well as in Chiang Mai.

NOVEMBER/DECEMBER

River Kwai Bridge Week: The famous Bridge on the River Kwai and the "Death Railway" are the venues for this festival at Kanchanaburi, featuring rides on old steam trains and impressive firework displays with light and sound shows on the bridge.

NATIONAL HOLIDAYS

1 Jan	New Year's Day
full moon in February	
	Makha Pucha
6 April	Chakri Day
13–15 April	*Songkran* (Thai New Year))
1 May	Labour Day
full moon in May	
	Visakha Pucha
full moon in July	
	Asaha Pucha
day after full moon in July	
	Khaopansa (start of Buddhist Lent)
28 July	King Maha Vajralongkorn's birthday
12 Aug	Birthday of Queen Sirikit
13 Oct	Death of King Bhumibol
23 Oct	Death of King Chulalongkorn
5 Dec	Birthday of King Bhumibol
10 Dec	Constitution Day
31 Dec	New Year's Eve

LINKS, BLOGS, APPS & MORE

LINKS & BLOGS

bk.asia-city.com Comprehensive on-line magazine (updated daily) for Bangkok featuring event announcements, restaurant reviews and tips for day trips and nights out on the town

www.travelfish.org Specialises in inexpensive accommodation. Cheeky descriptions, praise as well as criticism. The coolest site for budget travellers

www.thailandqa.com The abbreviation *qa* stands for question and answer. Here's where you'll find questions and answers about life and travel in Thailand

www.amazing-thailand.com Everything at a glance for your holiday destination: facts, general info, travel...

www.thaivisa.com/forum Where is a good place to go for breakfast in Hua Hin? Who provides bicycle tours in Bangkok? If you have questions, this well-attended forum will have an already blogged answer

www.thailand-uk.com/forums Whether you're curious about politics or culture, hotel ratings or visa regulations, this forum has the information you need

www.hospitalityclub.org The club is "a worldwide web of friendly people". Over 1,000 members in Thailand alone are registered. You can stay overnight – for free – with registered members, get valuable tips or even take a walk around the block

www.thaizer.com Roy Cavanagh lives in Thailand and knows everything about the country and its people. Useful advice on dos and don'ts, health, transport, the language and much more. Blog which is updated regularly

whatsonsukhumvit.com Countless tips and advice for foodies and tattoo junkies, bikers and others exploring Thailand, not only around Sukhumvit Road in Bangkok

Regardless of whether you are still researching your trip or already in Thailand: these addresses will provide you with more information, videos and networks to make your holiday even more enjoyable.

www.tmd.go.th First-hand weather reports from the official Thai Government's weather services. Offers seven-day and four-week forecasts, weather warnings, ocean forecasts and other useful information

www.360cities.net Forget unfocused YouTube videos with uninteresting commentaries: Take a 360 degrees tour of Thailand with panoramic photos of beaches and temples to prepare for your visit

www.thaiwebsites.com What does the web know about Thailand? This website is a directory for English-language Thailand-related websites and also posts articles on current topics

VIDEOS

www.bangkokpost.com/vdo This English-language newspaper website has many informative videos reporting on travel destinations as well as news bulletins from Thailand

www.youtube.com/channel/UC7ohHG5zM5V7y-l7Eyqoisg/videos Two travel bloggers take you along on their adventures in Thailand to places like Ko Chang, Chiang Mai and Bangkok

APPS

Amazing Thailand App with information on the most significant tourist destinations and lovely pictures, but unfortunately the practical tips are often a bit outdated

Green Tourism A guide to eco-friendly travel destinations and resorts put together by the Tourism Authority of Thailand

Learn Thai – Phrasebook An easy-to-use language app with the most important conversation building blocks, which you can also play out loud

Wongnai Thais love food! This popular app makes it easy to find the right restaurant every time and eat where the locals love to go

ACCOMMODATION

Many hotels add an additional surcharge of 10 to 20 percent for the peak season between Christmas and New Year. During off-season expect a discount, especially when booking online. Always ask for a discount when booking directly at the place! Hotel rooms in Thailand are always double rooms and you pay the same price even if you are travelling solo. Room rates for package tours (flight and accommodation) are often significantly lower than by booking directly. It's worth doing a comparison.

More exclusive accommodation will charge a tax and service fee of up to 17 percent. When you make your booking, make sure that this fee is already included so there are no nasty surprises. Unfortunately, in Thailand it is a common practice for hotels to foist a compulsory, expensive dinner on their guests over Christmas and New Year.

RESPONSIBLE TRAVEL

It doesn't take a lot to be environmentally friendly whilst travelling. Don't just think about your carbon footprint whilst flying to and from your holiday destination but also about how you can protect nature and culture abroad. As a tourist it is especially important to respect nature, look out for local products, cycle instead of driving, save water and much more. If you would like to find out more about eco-tourism please visit: *www.ecotourism.org*

ARRIVAL

Bangkok's Suvarnabhumi airport (pronounced: *Soowannapoom* | *www.suvarnabhumiairport.com*) is a hub for Southeast Asia and is served by most European and Asian airlines. The flight from London is approx. 11 hours. Charter airlines also land on the island of Phuket *(www.phuketairportthai.com/en)*. Even during the December/January high season non-stop return flights from London to Bangkok with major airlines such as British Airways or Thai Airways are available for around £ 900 (US-$ 1,180); cheap return flights to Bangkok or Phuket with one stopover can be had for as little as £ 400 (US-$ 525). Shortly before Christmas, however, the prices sometimes spike.

The cheapest means of transport from the Bangkok and Phuket airports into the city and to the beaches are train (Bangkok, *www.bangkokairporttrain.com*), shuttle or mini bus or *Public Taxi*. A trip by taxi from Bangkok Airport to the city costs approx. 400–500 baht, and from Phuket Airport to Patong Beach around 800 baht. Taxi tickets are sold at fixed prices at counters or terminals.

BANKING & CREDIT CARDS

The Thai baht (THB) is divided into 100 satang. Coins in 1, 2, 5 and 10 baht denominations and 20, 50, 100, 500 and 1,000 baht notes are in circulation. 25 and 50 satang coins are usually only found as change in supermarkets. You can withdraw money with your normal debit card at all newer ATMs bearing the V Pay sign. You may encounter problems when you use the new V Pay chip cards in older

From arrival to weather

Your holiday from start to finish: the most important addresses and information for your Thailand trip

ATMs. Visa is accepted by all large banks; Mastercard/Eurocard is also widespread. With an American Express Card, you'll only get cash at the branches of the *Bangkok Bank*. All banks charge a fee of 180 baht per transaction for money withdrawals. Always have the UK telephone number of your card provider on hand. Many shops accept credit cards, but they tend to add a hefty – and illegal! – surcharge for the service. Tip: if you offer to pay ash, you can often negotiate a lower price. Many of the smarter stores, restaurants and hotels add a Value Added Tax (VAT) of 7 percent to the price. At other establishments it is simply *"VAT included"*. Thais do not consider it unfair to charge a "rich" foreigner higher prices. This not only applies to shopping at markets, but also hotels, zoos, museums, amusement parks etc. Even state-run institutions such as national parks operate on the two-tier pricing system.

CAR HIRE & DRIVING

All the large rental companies can be found in Thailand. A small car costs approx. 1400 baht per day (discount for longer rental periods). Make sure your insurance includes personal and property damage waivers. An international driver's license will be accepted by the car hire company but, according to the Foreign Office, it is not a valid document in Thailand. Driving is on the left, as in the UK. The speed limit on motorways is 120 km/h, but just 90 km/h on highways and national roads. The blood alcohol limit is 0.5 per mille. Thailand has one of the highest number of road fatalities. Always be prepared to react quickly and use the hard shoulder in an emergency. Do not expect the same road rules as in Europe to apply; drivers of buses and trucks seem to think they own the road and it could be fatal to insist otherwise. Be vigilant of other road users who may be driving at high speeds under the influence of drink or drugs. Avoid driving at night especially on festive holidays such as *Songkran* when the number of accidents rises exponentially. An alternative: a rental vehicle with a driver (for an eight-hour day an extra charge of only 550 baht is common).

CHILD PROTECTION

Do you have compassion? Do you buy flowers, chewing gum or cigarettes from

BUDGETING

Noodle soup	£0.50/$0.67–£1.30/$1.68 *for a bowl from the cook shop*
T-shirt	£2.57/$3.36–£4.29/$5.60 *from a street vendor*
Drinking water	£0.21/$0.28–£0.50/$0.67 *for a bottle (1 litre) from the supermarket-*
Bus fare	£1.72/$2.24–£2.57/$3.36 *minibus from Bang kok to Ayutthaya (approx. 43 miles)*
Petrol	£0.77/$1 *for a litre of super*
Massage	£7.70/$10 *for a one-hour massage on the beach*

children to show your generosity? The child protection organisation *Childwatch Phuket (www.childwatchphuket.org)* strongly advises against it: "The more people who buy from the children, the stronger the likelihood they will have to work until early the next morning." Children do not work at night in bar districts out of pure necessity; child labour is a highly organised business run by ruthless people.

CLIMATE, WHEN TO GO

In the "cool" seasons from November to February daily temperatures average 30°C, lower in the north. From March until May it can get as hot as 40°C/104°F. During the rainy season from May to October temperatures abate somewhat, but the humidity increases. The sea is at its calmest from December/January to March/April. Ko Samui feels the effects of the northeast monsoon from November/December to the middle of February. But the rainy season from July to October is not as hefty there, so the European spring to summer is a good season to travel to the islands in the Gulf of Thailand. Swimming in the ocean during the monsoon seasons can be fatal! The tourist industry markets the rainy season as the "Green Season" and offers good deals at this time of year, but this is not the time to plan a trip if you want to hit the beach.

CURFEW

The nightly curfew is set by the government at 1am, for selected nightlife districts at 2am.

CUSTOMS

No customs duties apply to items for personal use brought into the country. Foreign exchange in excess of 20,000 US dollars must be declared. Importing of illegal drugs, firearms and pornographic media is forbidden as well as e-cigarettes, vaporizers and accessories. A permit must be obtained for the export of Buddha statues and antiques from the *Fine Arts Department (tel. 0 22 25 26 25)* in Bangkok who will take care of the necessary paperwork for you. Numerous animal products and antique Buddha statues cannot be taken out at all.

Travellers returning to the EU have the following duty-free allowance: 200 cigarettes, 250 g of tobacco or 50 cigars, 2 litres of wine and 1 litre of spirits (over 22% alcohol), 500 g of coffee, 50 g of perfume, 250 ml of eau de toilette and other goods to a value of about £370. When entering the USA, goods to a value of $ 800 including 2 litres of alcoholic drinks are duty-free (see *www.cbp.gov* or *www.gov.uk/duty-free-goods* for all details). Counterfeit and fake brand goods may be brought into the UK for private use only; if you attempt to bring in more than one such item, the "excess" items may be confiscated by the UK customs.

DOMESTIC FLIGHTS

You can fly cheaply from Bangkok to nearly every major provincial city in Thailand. A flight to Phuket with Thai Airways *(www.thaiairways.com)* costs from approx. 3600 baht. Air Asia *(www.airasia.com),* Bangkok Airways *(www.bangkokair.com)* and Nok Air *(www.nokair.com)* or Thai Lion Air *(www.lionairthai.com)* will fly you to your holiday destination often for just over half that price.

ELECTRICITY

The voltage is 220 volts. In the province, some places still use plugs with flat prongs. You can purchase an adaptor at electrical stores and *7 eleven* mini markets.

EMBASSIES

UK EMBASSY

14 Wireless Rd | Lumpini, Pathumwan | Bangkok 10330 | tel. 0 23 05 83 33 | www. ukinthailand.fco.gov.uk | Mon–Thu 8am– 4.30pm; Fri 8am–1 pm

US EMBASSY

95 Wireless Rd | Bangkok 10330 | tel. 0 22 05 40 00 | th.usembassy.gov | Mon– Fri 7am–4pm

HEALTH

Vaccinations are not mandatory, but some are recommended. In jungle regions near Myanmar and Cambodia there is a low but significant risk of malaria, which should not put yoou off a trekking tour. Information about malaria prophylaxis: Department of Health *(www.dh.gov.uk)*; National Travel Health Network and Centre *(www. nathnac.org)*; Malaria Reference Laboratory (MRL) *(www.malaria-reference. co.uk)*. Dengue fever and chikungunya fever are transmitted by day-active mosquitoes throughout the country. Wear bright, long-sleeved clothing and use sprays and coils to protect against bites. Engaging in unprotected sex puts you at considerable risk of contracting a sexually transmitted disease or becoming infected with HIV. Tap water is not safe to drink, but can be used for brushing your teeth. The standard of hygiene in Thailand is generally good. Additional health tips are available at the above websites. Many doctors and dentists practising in Bangkok and tourist centres will have been trained in Europe or America. Private hospitals in particular may well have better standards of service, and at a cheaper price, than in the West. Many independent doctors and dentists also

provide a high standard of care. All hospitals provide 24-hour emergency services. As there is no national system for emergency medical assistance, you have

CURRENCY CONVERTER

£	THB	THB	£
1	42	10	0.24
3	125	30	0.72
5	209	50	1.20
13	544	130	3.11
40	1,673	400	9.56
75	3,137	750	17.93
120	5,018	1200	28.69
250	10,456	2500	59.78
500	20,911	5000	119.56

$	THB	THB	$
1	32	10	0.31
3	96	30	0.94
5	160	50	1.56
13	416	130	4.06
40	1,280	400	12.49
75	2,400	750	23.42
120	3,840	1200	37.48
250	8,000	2500	78.08
500	16,000	5000	156.15

For current exchange rates see www.xe.com

to call the hospitals directly and request ambulance service. It is a good idea to book travel health insurance which includes your flight home in an emergency.

IMMIGRATION

For a visit not exceeding 30 days, visitors from many countries, including the UK, do not need a visa to enter Thailand, just a passport valid for at least 6 months. If you plan to stay more than a month, obtain a 60-day visa at a Thai consulate or embassy in your country before leaving home. Check *www.thaivisa.com* or the websites of Thailand's immigration *(www.immigration.go.th)* and the Ministry of Foreign Affairs *(www.mfa.go.th)* for details.

DIPLOMATIC REPRESENTATION

UK: *Royal Thai Embassy in London | 29–30 Queen's Gate | London SW7 5JB | tel. 030 79 48 10 | www.thaiembassyuk.org.uk*
US: *Royal Thai Embassy in Washington | 1024 Wisconsin Ave. | N.W. Washington D.C. 20007 | tel. 202 9 44 36 00 | www.thaiembdc.org*

INTERNET ACCESS & WIFI

Internet cafés are becoming a rarity in thailand, but they are cheap (about 20 baht per hour for access). In many restaurants and almost hotels, you can go online via WiFi with our own device. Obtaining the password is sometimes very expensive in big hotels; most of the time it is now free. It is definitely easier and cheaper to use your own smartphone with a Thai SIM card to go on-line. You can easily buy one in any *7-eleven* mini market (bring your passport!).

MEDIA

The English-language dailies "Bangkok Post" *(www.bangkokpost.com)* and "The Nation" *(www.nationmultimedia.com)* are available at most hotels and airports as well as newsstands. Free English-language weekly "BK Magazine" *(bk.asia-city.com)* and monthly "Bangkok 101" have good listings and reviews of sights, restaurants and happenings in the capital. The tourist centres carry leading foreign newspapers and magazines.

Most leading hotels provide satellite TV channels, which usually include CNN, CNBC and BBC.

MOTORCYCLES

The mountains of the north with their curvy roads and slopes are both a challenge and an unforgettable experience for bikers. For everything you need to know about motorcycle tours in this area, check out *www.gt-rider-com*. However, motorcycling is dangerous in Thailand. Three quarters of all fatal road accidents in the country involve motorcyclists. Amongst these casualties are tourists despite the legal obligation to wear a helmet. Insurance coverage is inadequate and an ambulance is usually slow to arrive at the accident scene. The fact that almost every visitor to Thailand insists on riding a moped without ever having tried it before does not make the roads any safer.

PHONE & MOBILE PHONE

The dialling code for the UK is 00144, for the US 001, for Australia 0061; dial the local area code without the zero. The international dialling code for Thailand is 0066; then dial the local number without the zero. In Thailand the area code must be dialled even for local calls: these are the first two (Bangkok) or first three (province) digits of the telephone numbers given in this guide.

The roaming fees are steep. Telephone calls made from hotel rooms are also very costly and it's advisable to get friends and relatives in the UK to call you back in your room over cheap call-by-call or call-through numbers. If you choose not to use WhatsApp or Skype for free international calling, the cheapest way is to purchase a Thailand SIM card for which you will receive your own telephone number (only useful if your mobile's SIM card locking function is not enabled). These top-up cards are available at various shops including all *7-Eleven* stores. You will only have to register once with your passport. Calling direct to the UK or USA from your mobile phone can be expensive, but the Thai mobile phone companies offer calling cards and prefixes with much better rates. Major companies include True Move *(truemoveh. truecorp.co.th)*, AIS *(www.ais.co.th)* and DTAC *(www.dtac.co.th)*.

PHOTOGRAPHY

Before photographing people, it's advisable to ask their permission – with a smile, in particular if you wish to photograph Muslim Thais.

POST

Airmail to Europe up to 10 g costs 17 baht, postcards 15 baht. Delivery time is usually between five and seven days. Postage for parcels is determined according to weight and mode of transportation (by ship or airplane). Airmail packages with a weight of 10 kg cost 4250 baht. Most post offices sell standard packages..

PUBLIC TRANSPORT

Trains are the safest and most popular means of transport in Thailand. Make sure you book a seat in advance, especially if you're travelling on festive holidays. There are also combo tickets available to take you to the islands, for example you can travel by train and then ferry to Ko Samui. The railway lines go

USEFUL PHRASES THAI

Letters in *italics* (masculine form) are to be replaced by the respective feminine form *[…]*, as necessary.

Yes/No	*krap [kah]* chai/mai chai	ครับ(ค่ะ) ใช่/ไม่ใช่
Please/Thank you	khaw … noy/khop koon *krab [kah]*	ขอ...หน่อย/ขอบคุณครับ(ค่ะ)
Sorry	khaw toht	ขอโทษ !
Good afternoon!/evening!	sahwadee *krab [kah]*	สวัสดีครับ(ค่ะ)
Goodbye	sahwadee	สวัสดี !
My name is …	chan joo …	ฉันชื่อ …
I'm from …	chan ma jag …	ฉันมาจาก ……
I don't understand you	chan mai khao jai koon	ฉันไม่เข้าใจคุณ
How much is …?	nee laka taolai	นี่ราคาเท่าไร ?
Excuse me, where can I find …?	khaw toht *krab [kah]* … yuu tee nai	ขอโทษครับ(ค่ะ) … อยู่ที่ไหน ?

1 nueng	หนึ่ง	5 hah	ห้า	9 gao	เก้า
2 song	สอง	6 hok	หก	10 sip	สิบ
3 sahm	สาม	7 jet	เจ็ด	20 yee sip	ยี่สิบ
4 see	สี่	8 beht	แปด	100 nueng loi	หนึ่งร้อย

from Bangkok to the north, to the northeast up to the Laos border, east to Pattaya, west to Kanchanaburi and beyond and south to Malaysia. Train timetables and fares: *www.railway.co.th.*

Direct buses take you from Bangkok to every large city in the country. Fares vary depending on the features and size of the bus as well as the class you're travelling in, but they are cheaper than in the UK. The air-conditioned "VIP" buses are quite comfortable and are fitted with sleeper seats (approx. 900 baht from Bangkok to Phuket). Remember to take a sweater and earplugs (to drone out the loud-playing videos) with you. Mini buses are generally faster but can be a hair-raising experience. Fares and booking: *12go.asia*. Car ferries (e.g. to Ko Samui, *www.rajaferryport.com)* and the many express boats and speedboats are perfect for island-hopping in the Andaman Sea and the Gulf of Thailand. During the monsoon season between May and October, boat travel can be interrupted due to high sea levels. Longtail fishing boats also charter passengers to 120 of the smaller islands. Sometimes you may need to hop off the ferry and onto a fishing boat for the last stage of your journey.

SAFETY

The *Tourist Police* is responsible for tourists and can be reached by phone nationwide: *tel. 11 55.* Most incidents involve cases of extortion by the local taxi and jet ski mafia (the majority of them based on Phuket) or drug abuse at full-moon parties (see p. 144). Cases are often reported of tourists, especially young women, unknowingly taking drugs so be careful of accepting drinks. Women should never find themselves alone on the beach at night. Unfortunately, there have been reports of scams and extortion by corrupt police for petty crimes. If you find yourself in this situation, contact your consulate immediately. The remaining tricksters, who include tuk-tuk drivers, self-appointed mendicants and English teachers, are harmless once your common sense tells you that something isn't right. Since the repeated bomb attacks in 2015–2017 and the increase in crime-related incidents (theft, robbery, rape especially on Phuket and Ko Samui as well as in Pattaya), the Foreign Office advises visitors to be particularly vigilant *(www.gov.uk/government/organisations/ foreign-commonwealth-office).*

SMOKING BAN

There is a strict smoking ban in place in public places and restaurants, bars and clubs and since January 2018, this also applies to 24 beaches, including the popular Patong Beach on Phuket, Hua Hin and Khao Lak. Offences carry a fine of 100,000 baht!

TAXI

So-called *Meter Taxis,* which have their fare meter switched on, are only available in Bangkok and in Phuket at the airport. Everywhere else the price must be negotiated – before you embark on your journey! The first kilometre in a *Meter Taxi* costs 35 baht, and every additional kilometre 6 Baht. For these prices it is almost impossible – at least for a tourist – to hire a three-wheel Tuk Tuk. Drivers often demand extortionate prices from tourists. If you insist on taking a tuk-tuk, first inquire at the hotel reception to have a rough idea of what the average price of a journey costs, then flag one down (do not wait for them to address you and do not flag one down in front of the hotel) and then negotiate the price, preferably in Thai.

TIME

Thailand time is GMT plus 7 hours throughout the year (New York plus 14 hours, Australia minus 3 hours).

TIPPING & SERVICE CHARGES

Tipping is not commonplace in average restaurants or at food stands. The higher quality restaurants will add a service charge of 10 percent to your bill (17 percent including taxes). In restaurants that don't add the service charge, but have provided good service, a 10 percent tip is appropriate. Bear in mind that porters and other service staff as well as nice taxi drivers are grateful for a small gratuity (e.g. the change).

TOURIST INFORMATION

THAILAND TOURIST AUTHORITY
UK: 17–19 Cockspur Street | London SW1Y 5BL | tel. 0870 900 2007
US: Broadway, Suite 2810 | New York, NY 10006 | tel. 212/432-0433

TOURISM AUTHORITY OF THAILAND (TAT)
The Tourism Authority of Thailand has offices in all major provincial capitals. Addresses for various offices are found in the chapters for the different regions, and e-mail addresses are listed on the website *www.tourismthailand.org.* You can find a wealth of information about Thailand on the Internet*: www.thaiwebsites.com, www.amazing-thailand.com,* and *www. sawadee.com.* Weather information can be found at *www.tmd.go.th/en*

WEATHER IN BANGKOK

	Jan	Feb	March	April	May	June	July	Aug	Sept	Oct	Nov	Dec
Daytime temperatures in °C/°F	32/90	33/91	34/93	35/95	34/93	33/91	32/90	32/90	32/90	31/88	31/88	31/88
Nighttime temperatures in °C/°F	20/68	23/73	24/75	26/79	25/77	25/77	25/77	24/75	24/75	23/73	23/73	20/68
Sunshine hours/day	8	8	8	10	8	6	5	5	5	6	7	8
Precipitation days/month	1	2	3	4	13	14	15	15	17	13	4	1
Water temperature in °C/°F	26/79	27/81	27/81	28/82	28/82	28/82	28/82	28/82	28/82	27/81	27/81	27/81

ROAD ATLAS

The green line indicates the Discovery Tour "Thailand at a glance"
The blue line indicates the other Discovery Tours

All tours are also marked on the pull-out map

Photo: Rice field at Chiang Mai

Exploring Thailand

The map on the back cover shows how the area has been sub-divided

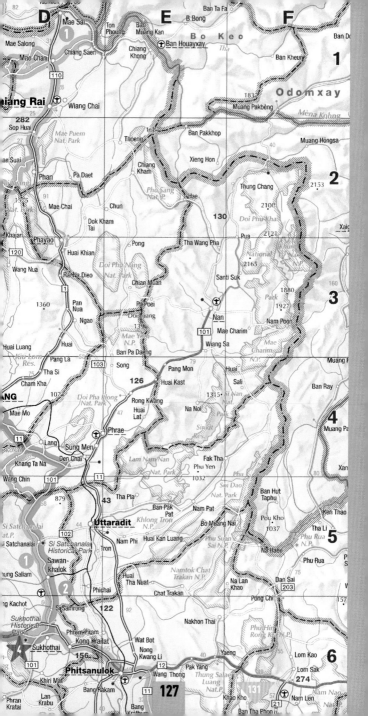

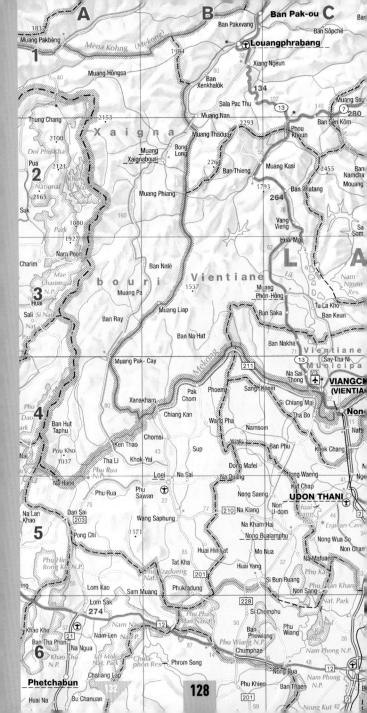

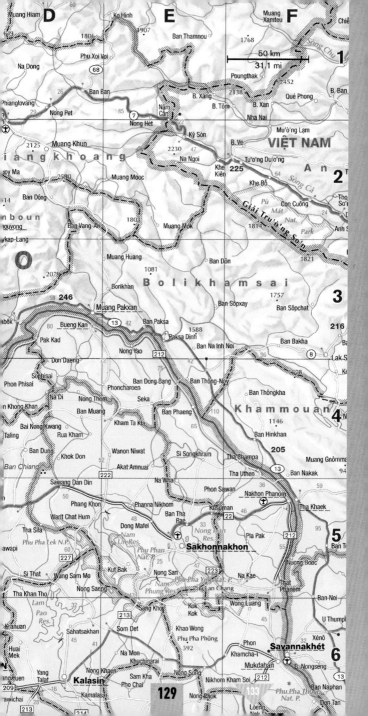

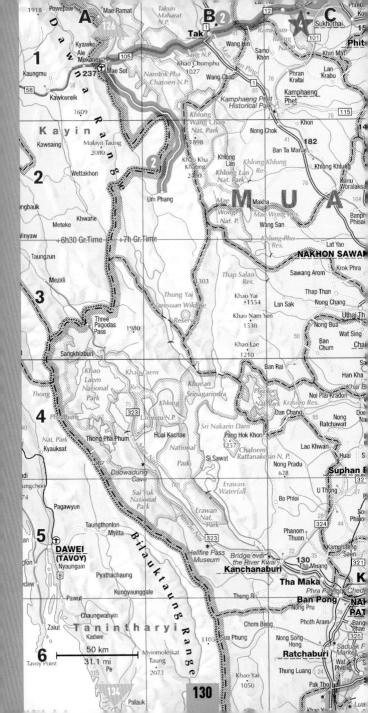

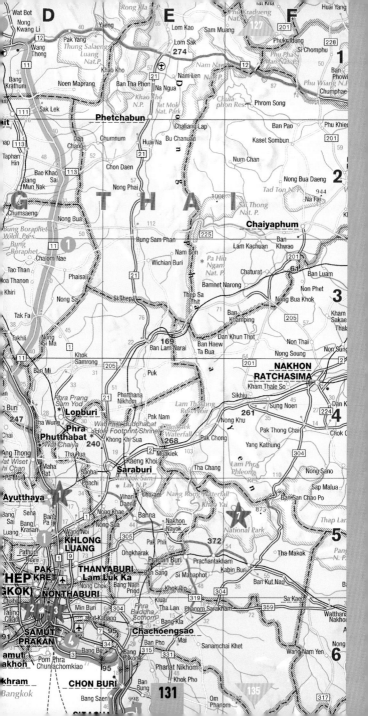

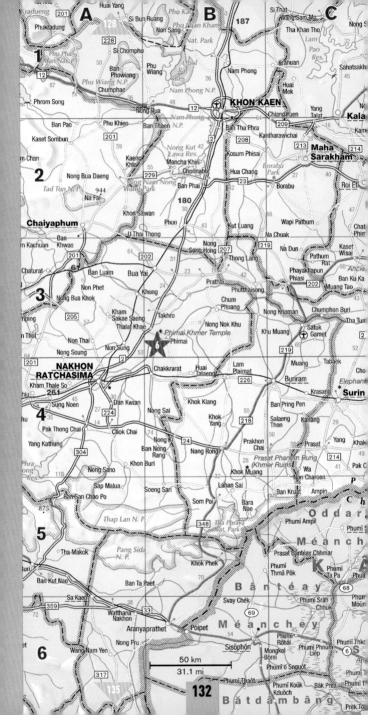

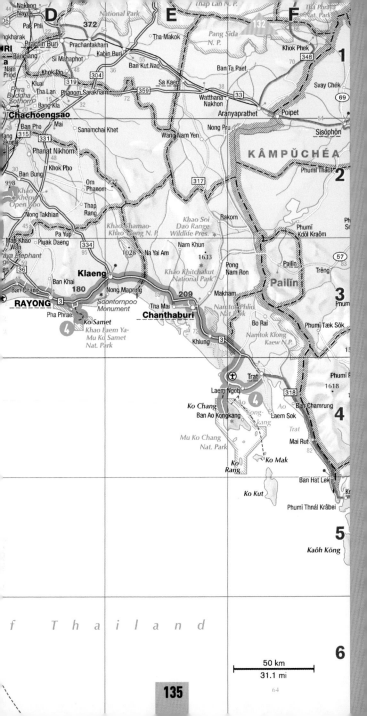

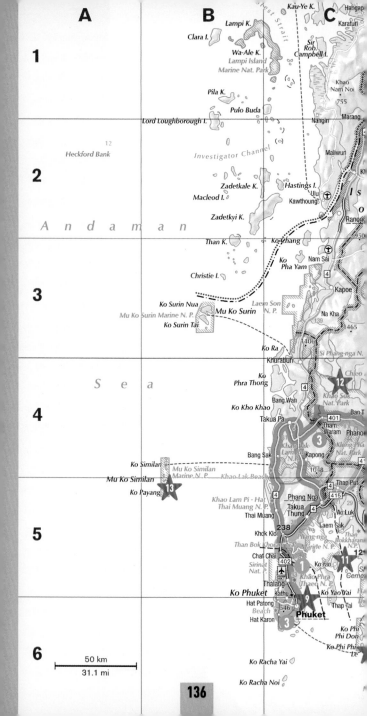

A

1

B
Lampi K.
Clara I.
Wa-Ale K.
*Lampi Island
Marine Nat. Park*
Pila K.
Pulo Buda
Lord Loughborough I.

C
Kau-Ye K.
Hangan
Karatun
Sir
Rob.
Campbell I.
Khao
Nam Noi
755
Nangin
Marang

2

Heckford Bank
12

Investigator Channel
Zadetkale K.
Macleod I.
Zadetkyi K.
Hastings I.
Ulu
Kawthoung
Maliwun
K
I S
o
Ranor

A   n   d   a   m   a   n

3

Than K.
Ko Chang
Ko
Pha Yam
Nam Sai
4
Kapoe
Na Kha
1465
Christie I.
Laem Son
N. P.
Si Phang-nga N.
Ko Surin Nua
Mu Ko Surin Marine N. P.
Mu Ko Surin
Ko Surin Tai
Ko Ra
1106
139

4

S   e   a
Khuraburi
Ko
Phra Thong
Bang Wan
Ko Kho Khao
Takua Pa
Bang Sak
Ko Similan
*Mu Ko Similan
Marine N. P.*
Mu Ko Similan
Ko Payang
Khao Lak Beach
Chuo
⭐12
*Khao Sok
Nat. Park*
Ban T
Tham
Waram
Phano
③
Kapong
*Kloeng Ha
Nat. Park*
4
4
401
1048

5

*Khao Lam Pi - Hat
Thai Muang N. P.*
Thai Muang
Khok Kloi
Than Bok Khoo
Chat Chai
*Sirinat
Nat.*
Thalang
Kathu
Ko Phuket
Hat Patong
Beach
Hat Karon
⭐13
Phang Nga
Takua
Thung
4
④
Laem Sak
238
*Phang-nga
Marine N. P.*
Ko Yao
Ko Yao Yai
546
Thap Put
415
4
*Than
Bokkharani
N. P.*
Ao Luk
29
12
⭐11
S
Geme
⭐9
Phuket
③
Ko Yao Noi
Thap Tai
①
⭐
402
*Khao Phra
Thaeo N. P.*

6

50 km
31.1 mi
Ko Racha Yai
Ko Racha Noi
Ko Phi
Phi Don
Ko Phi Phi
Te

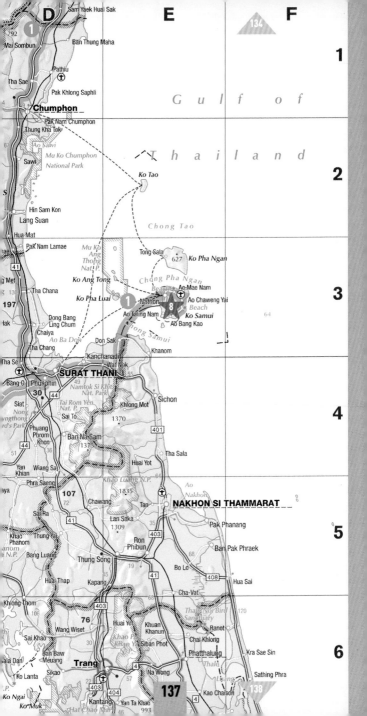

134

Sam Yaek Huai Sak

792

Mai Sombun

Ban Thung Maha

Pathiu

Tha Sae

Pak Khlong Saphli

Chumphon

Pak Nam Chumphon

Thung Kha Tok

Ao Sawi

Mu Ko Chumphon
National Park

Gulf of

Thailand

Sawi

Ko Tao

Hin Sam Kon

Lang Suan

Chong Tao

Hua Mat

Pak Nam Lamae

41

Mu Ko
Ang
Thong
Nat'l P.

Tong Sala

627

Ko Pha Ngan

g Met

8 130

197

Ko Ang Tong

Chong Pha Ngan

Beach

Ao Mae Nam

Ko Pha Luai

Nathon

Ao Chaweng Yai

Beach

lak

Dong Bang
Ling Chum

Ao Taling Nam

Ko Samui

Ao Bang Kao

64

Chaiya

Chong Samui

Tha Chang

Don Bang
Ling Chum

Don Sak

Tha Se

Kanchanadit

Khanom

Bang O

SURAT THANI

Wat Nok

Phunphin

30

44

Namtok Si Khit
Nat. Park

49

Siat

Nong
ngthong
rd's Park

Tai Rom Yen
Nat. P.

Sai To

Khlong Mot

Sichon

Phuang
Phrom
Khon

Ban Na Sam

1370

401

44

137

36

Yan
Khian

Wiang Sa

Phra Saeng

Huai Yot

Tha Sala

107

Khao Luang N.P.

Ao
Nakhon

72

Chawang

1835

NAKHON SI THAMMARAT

Khao
Phanom
anom
N.P.

Sai Ra

Lan Saka

Tan

1309

35

Pak Phanang

41

403

Bang Luang

Ron
Phibun

Ban Pak Phraek

Thung Yai

Thung Song

19

Bo Lo

68

408

Huai Thap

Kapang

41

Cha-Vat

Hua Sai

Khlong Thom

403

Thale Noi Bird
Sanctuary

120

106

76

Huai Yot

Khuan
Khanun

Ranot

Wang Wiset

30

Khao P
Khao Ya

Siban Phot

Chai Khlong

Kra Sae Sin

Sai Khao

Ban Baw
Meuang

Chai Khlong

Phatthalung

Thale

Sikao

Trang

4

Na Wong

138

Sathing Phra

la Dan

Ko Lanta

403

404

Yan Ta Khao

Kao Chaison

4

Ko Ngai

Kantang

993

Hat Chao Mai

Ko Muk

137

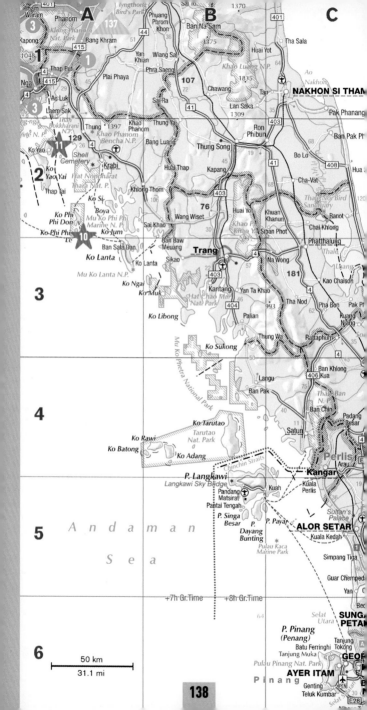

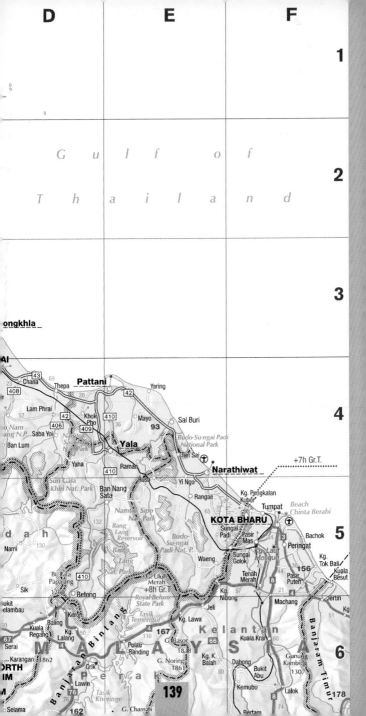

D E F

1

Gulf of

2

Thailand

3

ongkhla

Pattani
Chana 43 69
408 23 Thepa 42 20
Lam Phrai 52
42 Mayo Sai Buri
Khok 406 409 410 36 93
Pho Yala Budo-Su-ngai Padi National Park
Saba Yoi
Nam ang N.P. Ban Lum Ten Sai
Yaha Raman **Narathiwat** +7h Gr.T.
Sun Gala Khiri Nat. Park Adso Yi Ngo
Ban Nang Sata Rangae Kg. Pengkalan Kubor
Namtu Sipo N. Park Beach Chinta Berahi
Bang Lang Reservoir 65 Tumpat
d a h Bang Lang Nat. Park **KOTA BHARU** Bachok
Nami 130 Sungai Padi Kg. Laut Mosque Peringat
Budo-Su-ngai Padi Nat. P. Pasir Mas 3
Waeng Sungai Golok Kg. Tok Bali
Bt Tata Papajing 410 Tenah Merah 156
Slk 120 Ulu Merah Kuala Besut
ukit elambau Betong Royal-Belum State Park Kg. Nibong Pasir Puteh Jertih
Baling Tasik Temengur Jeli Machang
Kuala Regang Kg. Lalang Kg. Lawa Banjaran Timur
67 Serai 4 Pulau 167 Kelantan 51
Karangan 1862 Grik Banding 66 Kuala Krai 60 Kg
ORTH IM Lawin 76 G. Noring 186 Kg. K. Balah Dahong Gunung Kambing 130
M Selama 162 Tasik Kneringe **139** Bukit Abu
G. Chamah Kemubu Lalok 178
Bertam 74

4

5

6

KEY TO ROAD ATLAS

Autobahn, mehrspurige Straße - in Bau Highway, multilane divided road - under construction	═══ ═ ═ ═	Autoroute, route à plusieurs voies - en construction Autosnelweg, weg met meer rijstroken - in aanleg
Fernverkehrsstraße - in Bau Trunk road - under construction	━━━ ─ ─ ─	Route à grande circulation - en construction Weg voor interlokaal verkeer - in aanleg
Hauptstraße Principal highway		Route principale Hoofdweg
Nebenstraße Secondary road		Route secondaire Overige verharde wegen
Fahrweg, Piste Practicable road, track		Chemin carrossable, piste Weg, piste
Straßennummerierung Road numbering	E20 11 70 26 5 40 9	Numérotage des routes Wegnummering
Entfernungen in Kilometer Distances in kilometers	**259** 130 ⎯ 129	Distances en kilomètres Afstand in kilometers
Höhe in Meter - Pass Height in meters - Pass	1365 •	Altitude en mètres - Col Hoogte in meters - Pas
Eisenbahn - Eisenbahnfähre Railway - Railway ferry	━━━ ··········	Chemin de fer - Ferry-boat Spoorweg - Spoorpont
Autofähre - Schifffahrtslinie Car ferry - Shipping route		Bac autos - Ligne maritime Autoveer - Scheepvaartlijn
Wichtiger internationaler Flughafen - Flughafen Major international airport - Airport	✈ ✈	Aéroport importante international - Aéroport Belangrijke internationale luchthaven - Luchthaven
Internationale Grenze - Provinzgrenze International boundary - Province boundary		Frontière internationale - Limite de Province Internationale grens - Provinciale grens
Unbestimmte Grenze Undefined boundary		Frontière d'Etat non définie Rijksgrens onbepaalt
Zeitzonengrenze Time zone boundary	-4h Greenwich Time ••••••••••• -3h Greenwich Time	Limite de fuseau horaire Tijdzone-grens
Hauptstadt eines souveränen Staates National capital	**MANILA**	Capitale nationale Hoofdstad van een souvereine staat
Hauptstadt eines Bundesstaates Federal capital	**Kuching**	Capitale d'un état fédéral Hoofdstad van een deelstat
Sperrgebiet Restricted area		Zone interdite Verboden gebied
Nationalpark National park		Parc national Nationaal park
Antikes Baudenkmal Ancient monument	∴	Monument antiques Antiek monument
Sehenswertes Kulturdenkmal Interesting cultural monument	∗ Angkor Wat	Monument culturel interéssant Bezienswaardig cultuurmonument
Sehenswertes Naturdenkmal Interesting natural monument	∗ Ha Long Bay	Monument naturel interéssant Bezienswaardig natuurmonument
Brunnen Well	‿	Puits Bron
MARCO POLO Erlebnistour 1 MARCO POLO Discovery Tour 1		MARCO POLO Tour d'aventure 1 MARCO POLO Avontuurlijke Routes 1
MARCO POLO Erlebnistouren MARCO POLO Discovery Tours		MARCO POLO Tours d'aventure MARCO POLO Avontuurlijke Routes
MARCO POLO Highlight	★1	MARCO POLO Highlight

MARCO POLO TRAVEL GUIDES

Travel with
Insider
Tips

INDEX

This index contains all places, excursion destinations and beaches featured in this guide. Page numbers in bold type refer to the main entry..

WRITE TO US

e-mail: info@marcopologuides.co.uk

Did you have a great holiday?
Is there something on your mind?
Whatever it is, let us know!
Whether you want to praise, alert us to errors or give us a personal tip – MARCO POLO would be pleased to hear from you.
We do everything we can to provide the very latest information for your trip.

Nevertheless, despite all of our authors' thorough research, errors can creep in. MARCO POLO does not accept any liability for this. Please contact us by e-mail or post.

MARCO POLO Travel Publishing Ltd
Pinewood, Chineham Business Park
Crockford Lane, Chineham
Basingstoke, Hampshire RG24 8AL
United Kingdom

PICTURE CREDITS
Cover Photograph: Krabi, Hat Tham Phra Nang Beach, Railay Beach (huber-images: B. Morandi)
Photographs: DuMont Bildarchiv: Sasse (4 top, 26/27, 62); © fotolia.com: Mike Thomas (18 centre); Wilfried Hahn (34, 58, 99, 111); huber-images: L. Debelkova (48), Gräfenhain (4 bottom, 86), F. Lukasseck (32/33), B. Morandi (1, 46/47), R. Schmid (89), Stadler (flap left), O. Stadler (2, 79), L. Vaccarella (29, 36/37), huber-images/Picture Finder (115); © iStockphoto/jabejon (18 bottom); M. Kirchgessner (112); K. Maeritz (68); mauritius images: Beck (113), Cassio (22), Vidier (8), Vidler (31), J. Warburton-Lee (107); mauritius images/age fotostock: D. Stamboulis (52); mauritius images/Alamy (3, 7, 9, 11, 18 top, 19 top, 28 left, 30, 30/31, 38, 41, 54, 56/57, 66, 70, 84/85, 103, 114 bottom, 128/129), L. Duggleby (91); mauritius images/Alamy/Arterra Picture Library (61); mauritius images/Alamy/Danita Delimont Creative (76); mauritius images/BlueHouseProject (92/93); mauritius images/Imagebroker: J. Beck (72), D. Bleyer (50), S. Grassegger (19 bottom), K. Landwer-Johan (12/13), O. Stadler (64/65), M. Wolf (43); mauritius images/Imagebroker/GTW (44); mauritius images/McPHOTO (71); mauritius images/SuperStock (10); mauritius images/Westend61: R. Richter (108/109); mauritius images/Alamy (6); mauritius images/Prisma (104/105); O. Stadler (flap right, 14/15, 20/21, 28 right, 74/75, 81, 82, 112/113, 114 top); O. Stadler/A. Stubhan (25); T. Stankiewicz (17); White Star: Reichelt (5)

3rd Edition – fully revised and updated 2020
Worldwide Distribution: Marco Polo Travel Publishing Ltd, Pinewood, Chineham Business Park, Crockford Lane, Basingstoke, Hampshire RG24 8AL, United Kingdom. Email: sales@marcopolouk.com
Author: Wilfried Hahn; co-author: Martina Miethig; editor: Felix Wolf
What's hot: wunder media, Munich; Mischa Loose; Martina Miethig
Cartography road atlas: © MAIRDUMONT, Ostfildern; Cartography pull-out map: © MAIRDUMONT, Ostfildern
Design front cover, p. 1, pull-out map cover: Karl Anders – Büro für Visual Stories, Hamburg; interior: milchhof:atelier, Berlin; Discovery Tours, p. 2/3: Susan Chaaban Dipl.-Des. (FH).
Translated by Susan Jones, Tübingen; Prepress: writehouse, Cologne
Phrase book in cooperation with Ernst Klett Sprachen GmbH, Stuttgart, Editorial by Pons Wörterbücher

MIX
Paper from responsible sources
FSC® C124385

DOS & DON'TS

Some things are best avoided in Thailand

DON'T DISPLAY ANGER

On rare occasions, the otherwise self-controlled Thai can become volatile, especially if alcohol is involved. Politely decline an invitation to a night out on the town by anyone you're not acquainted with, or simply excuse yourself after one drink. If you start to feel aggressive, stay calm. Also avoid inciting an already angry local to lose face.

DON'T INSULT THE KING

Lese-majeste is liable to prosecution and can have serious repercussions, even for tourists. In 2009, Australian author Harry Nicolaides was sentenced to three years in prison for defaming the then crown prince and today's king, Maha Vajiralongkorn, in his book. Although his father, king Bhumibol Adulyadej, who died in 2016, personally pardoned him, Nicolaides had to spend six months in a Thai prison.

DON'T USE DRUGS

Although Thailand carries the death penalty for drug trafficking, it is not unlikely that you will be offered some type of narcotic, for example, at the notorious full moon parties on Ko Phangan. But be careful: even the smallest trace of drugs such as *ganja* (marijuana) can end up sending you to prison!

DON'T MESS AROUND WITH THE SCOOTER MAFIA

Racing over the waves on a water scooter or jet ski might sound like innocent holiday fun, but there are some hidden dangers. Not only are these loud gas guzzlers a danger to swimmers and snorkelers, but also the locals who rent them out have a worse reputation than the so-called tuk-tuk mafia known for ripping off tourists. It is quite common for them to insist on a huge amount of money to compensate for supposed damages to the scooters, sometimes even with threats of violence.

DON'T FOLLOW TOUTS

Touts lurk wherever there are tourists. They offer everything under the sun: gemstones, free sightseeing tours, prostitutes. As a rule, Thais act reserved around tourists and are not inclined to accost them on the street. If you are approached by a local, chances are you could be the target of a scam.

DON'T TRAVEL IN THE DEEP SOUTH

Pattani, Yala and Narathiwat are the three southernmost provinces. The majority of the population is Muslim. Attacks in this region occur often, and since 2004 an estimated 6000 people have died as a result of the clashes. Terrorists want to force independence from Thailand. Avoid this crisis area!